Don't Check Your Brains At The Door

JOSH McDOWELL
& BOB HOSTETLER

WORD PUBLISHING

Dallas · London · Vancouver · Melbourne

DON'T CHECK YOUR BRAINS AT THE DOOR

Library of Congress Cataloging-in-Publication Data

McDowell, Josh.
    Don't check your brains at the door / Josh McDowell and Bob Hostetler.
       p.   cm.
    Summary: Examines common myths about God, religion, and life that contradict God's Word.
    ISBN 0–8499–3234–3 :
    1. Youth—Religious life. 2. Witness bearing (Christianity) [1. Christian life. 2. Conduct of life.] I. Hostetler, Bob, 1958–. II. Title. III. Title: Do not check your brains at the door.
BV4531.M217   1992
239—dc20
                                     91–44765
                                         CIP
                                          AC

Printed in the United States of America
8 9 QBP 22 21 20

Contents

Myths About the Bible

Myths About the Resurrection

Myths About Religion and Christianity

Contents

Myths About Life and Happiness

Acknowledgments

When one of my books is published, it is generally the result of a team of dedicated people to whom I am personally indebted. And this book is no exception. I am indebted to Joey Paul of Word Publishing, who introduced us to Bob Hostetler, my co-author; to Dave Bellis for working with Bob to mold and shape the book into its final form; and especially to Bob Hostetler himself. It has been a privilege and an honor to work with such a creative and talented man as Bob. His insights, humor, and gifted writing ability have ministered to me as I'm sure they will minister to you. While this book has been a cooperative effort, Bob deserves the real credit.

Josh McDowell

"We" Versus "I"

The personal experiences in this book are from both my life and the life of Bob Hostetler. We thought it would make it easier to read and be less confusing to refer to these in the first person rather than try to identify which of us experienced them.

Josh

Introduction

They called him the Picasso of counterfeiting.

He was the best. His skill at making phony money was legendary. And he had labored for a full year to perfect the finest set of counterfeit engraving plates ever created.

When he was caught, this artist challenged the government agents who arrested him. He placed one of his own counterfeit $20 bills beside the bill he had copied. "I defy you," he said, "to tell the difference between these two bills!"

The Treasury man didn't argue.

"I don't have to," he said. "The one you copied is fake, too."

A lot of Christian teenagers today make the same mistake. They carefully duplicate the beliefs of their parents. They reflect the opinions of their friends. They assimilate the values they see displayed in society. They mimic the behavior they observe at church. Tragically, though, many of the things they copy are counterfeits themselves, like the unfortunate counterfeiter.

Annie is amazed at the reaction she gets when she proposes the Bible be included on a reading list for a college course in world literature. "You can't be serious," some people say. "The Bible may have some fascinating myths and legends, but don't ask me to take it seriously."

Sixteen-year-old Samantha unthinkingly accepts the common view that "Christians, Buddhists, Muslims—it doesn't much matter, y'know? It's like we all want to go to heaven, we're just taking different roads to the same place."

When it comes to boy/girl relationships, Ken has a locker-room mentality. "You're not a man until you've 'done it'!"

He views sex as a rite of passage, the line where a boy becomes a man.

Stephanie's showdown with her parents reveals one of her convictions. "You can't tell me what's right and what's wrong," she insists. "I'm almost eighteen. You can't push your morals off on me. Just because it's wrong for you doesn't mean it's wrong for me."

So what's truth and what's myth? Teenagers and young adults get it from every direction: their parents tell them one thing and friends say the opposite. Hollywood preaches one message; the church says, "No, that's wrong." Some of that is truth. Much of it is myth.

That's what this book is all about. These brief chapters discuss common myths, many of which people accept without thinking, and evaluate them in the light of the Bible. It will surprise, delight, and sometimes scare you to discover some deeply held ideas about God and religion and life that are no more than myths.

Each chapter concludes with a quick workout, a short exercise that builds on the material in the chapter and provides a crucial perspective from God's Word.

The authors hope that when you have confronted the myths in these pages, you will "be ready always to give an answer to every man that asketh you a reason of the hope that is in you" (1 Peter 3:15 KJV). Not only that, but your faith may be strengthened to the point that you'll also be armed to confront other previously unchallenged lies that contradict or dilute the truth of God's Word.

Myths About God

1
The Cosmic Cop

Exposing the Killjoy Myth

Many people imagine God as a cosmic cop standing in the center of the galaxies like a policeman directing traffic.

"Hey, you! Yeah, you. You look like you're having fun over there. Well, cut it out!"

"And you, with the videotape. What's it rated? R? PG-13? Hand it over, slow and easy like!"

"And who's that couple liplocked in that dark corner? That you, Cindy? And Robert—I shoulda known. We'll have no more of that. Not while I'm patrolling this beat."

God. The Cosmic Killjoy. All we want to do is have a little fun. God just wants to spoil it for us.

Conversely, we imagine the devil as a fun-loving imp. Comedian Flip Wilson popularized the phrase, "The devil made me do it," as if the devil is a "good ol' boy" who only wants to help us enjoy ourselves.

That's a lie.

The devil doesn't care if you have fun. He hates your guts. He will eat you up. Peter says that the devil is always "seeking whom he may devour."

A group of tourists in the Holy Land were told by their guide, "You're probably used to seeing shepherds in your country driving sheep through fields and roads. But in Palestine things are different; the shepherd always leads the way, going before the flock."

Much to the amusement of the tourists, the first flock of sheep they saw was being driven, not led. Embarrassed, the guide asked the man, "How is it that you are driving these sheep? I've always understood that Eastern shepherds *lead* the sheep."

"Oh," replied the man. "That's true. The shepherd does lead his sheep. But I'm not the shepherd. I'm the butcher."

Satan is a butcher. He is not interested in giving you pleasure or happiness. He is only interested in devouring you.

Jesus put things in perspective and exploded this myth when He said, "The thief [Satan] comes only to steal and kill and destroy; I have come that [you might] have life, and have it to the full" (John 10:10).

The devil doesn't care if you have fun. He only wants to steal and kill and destroy you.

God does not want to spoil your fun. He wants you to enjoy life and enjoy it to the full. He wants you to experience a full and joyful life, the "eternal pleasures" that the psalmist talked about:

> You have made known to me the path of life;
> you will fill me with joy in your presence,
> with eternal pleasures at your right hand.
>
> *Psalm 16:11*

Workout

Increase your power to confront the Killjoy Myth with this workout:

Read 1 Peter 5:8. How does this verse portray Satan? Why?

Read Job 2:1–8. What does the devil want to happen to Job? Why?

Read Zechariah 3:1. What does Satan do for or to Joshua in this verse?

Read Revelation 12:10. This verse speaks of Satan. What does it say he does "day and night"? From what you read in Job and Zechariah, can you determine to whom "our brothers" refers? Does it include you?

2
The Luke Skywalker God

Exposing the Impersonal Force Myth

L uke Skywalker, having just escaped from the Sandpeople, stands in the spartan dwelling of Obi-Wan Kenobi on the planet of Tatooine. Luke has just learned that Obi-Wan was a Jedi Knight who had fought in the Clone Wars with Luke's father. Obi-Wan gives him a lightsaber that once belonged to Luke's father and, in the course of the conversation, mentions "the Force."

"The Force?" Luke says.

Obi-Wan responds, "Well, the Force is what gives the Jedi his power. It's an energy field created by all living things. It surrounds us and penetrates us. It binds the galaxy together."

That concept of the Force, which occurs throughout the immensely popular *Star Wars* movies, has a familiar ring to it. That is because "the Force" is what many people imagine God to be. They picture God as a faceless, formless "energy," an impersonal "force," that mysteriously surrounds and guides the universe.

But that's a myth.

Oh, God does surround and guide the universe. He is present everywhere. He is Spirit. But He is not some mysterious "force," not some elusive "energy" that's just "out there somewhere." He is not a "thing," an "it." The astounding thing about God is that He is a personal God.

"I love those who love me," He says, "and those who seek me find me" (Proverbs 8:17). Notice the personal pronouns God uses to refer to Himself. "I . . . me . . . me . . . me." Does that sound like some "cosmic energy?"

Far from being an impersonal force, God is referred to in the Bible as "the God of Abraham, Isaac, and Jacob." He told His name to Moses. He revealed Himself to the boy Samuel.

He spoke to Isaiah in the Temple. He told Jeremiah, "Before I formed you in the womb I knew you" (Jeremiah 1:5). The Apostle Paul called Him "my God." King David called Him "a father to the fatherless, a defender of widows." And all Christians have received the "spirit of sonship," so that we may call Him "Abba, Father" (Romans 8:15).

God, the true God, is *personally* interested in you. He knows your name. "See," He says to His people, "I have engraved you on the palms of my hands" (Isaiah 49:16). "He cares for you," the Apostle Peter says (1 Peter 5:7). Jesus says that "even the very hairs of your head are all numbered" (Matthew 10:30). And God promises that you can "call upon me and come and pray to me, and I will listen to you. You will seek me and find me when you seek me with all your heart" (Jeremiah 29:12–13). That's a promise you may take *personally*.

Workout

Increase your power to confront the Impersonal Force Myth with this workout:

Read Jeremiah 29:12–13 in the last paragraph of this chapter. Circle each personal pronoun ("I," "me," "you," etc.) in those verses.

Locate the portion of Jeremiah 1:5 quoted in the preceding chapter. Circle the personal pronouns in that brief reference.

Read Moses' encounter with God in Exodus 3:1–15. How does God identify Himself to Moses in verse 6? By what name does He call Himself in verse 14? How many times does God use the pronoun "I" in these verses (count them and write the answer here: _____).

3

The Vending
Machine God

Exposing the Father
Christmas Myth

Okay, God, I'm gonna give You a chance to prove Yourself."

Bob knelt beside his bed. He was seven years old and wanted fiercely to believe in God. So he bent his unruly red head over folded hands and continued.

"I really want to believe in You, God. So when I wake up in the morning, if there's a million dollars under my bed, I'll know You're real. And I'll never doubt You again."

He didn't get the million dollars.

Maybe it was because he wanted the money more than he desired God. Maybe, too, the money wasn't there in the morning because a million dollars (he expected it in one-dollar bills) wouldn't fit under the bed with the Monopoly game, GI Joe, record player, dirty clothes, and dust bunnies occupying so much space.

Probably, though, the reason he didn't get the money had more to do with a mistaken idea about God. Bob imagined God to be like a vending machine: you deposit a prayer, push the right button, and your wish is fulfilled. He imagined God to be a Father Christmas figure who waited in the uncharted expanse of space to fulfill his wish list. If he prayed hard enough and believed hard enough, God would plop down everything a seven-year-old heart desired.

That's understandable for a child. Unfortunately, many people carry their perceptions of God as a Divine Vending Machine into adulthood. They never advance beyond the Father Christmas Myth in their understanding of God.

God loves to answer prayer. He says, "Call to me and I will answer you" (Jeremiah 33:3). He even promises, "Before they call I will answer; while they are still speaking I will hear" (Isaiah 65:24).

But prayer is not a coin to be inserted in a vending machine, and faith is not a button you push. God does not submit to our whims and wishes. No matter how hard seven-year-old Bob prayed for that million dollars, no matter how fervently he believed, he would not have found it under the bed the next morning. Not because God doesn't love him. Not because God doesn't answer prayer. Not even because there was no room under the bed. The million bucks never came because Bob was not really praying; he was wishing.

Contrary to the Father Christmas Myth, God is not some heavenly vending machine for the dispensing of gifts and favors. He transcends our petty wishes. He is Almighty God, Love Incarnate. He longs for His children to return the love He has lavished upon them. He wants us to love *Him*, not things. He wants us to seek *Him*, not answers to greedy prayers. He wants us to obey Him, not because it might get us a million dollars, but because we love Him and want to please Him.

And, ironically, when we advance in knowledge beyond the image of the Vending Machine God, His Word promises that we can "have confidence before God and receive from him anything we ask, because we obey his commands and do what pleases him" (1 John 3:21–22).

Workout

Increase your power to confront the Father Christmas Myth with this workout:

Each of the following verses indicates a condition for answered prayer that can be expressed in one word. Write that word on the line beside the verse.

2 Chronicles 7:14 _____

Jeremiah 29:13 _____

Mark 11:24 _____

James 5:16 _____

1 John 5:14 _____

Myths About
Jesus

4
Prophet Jesus

Exposing the Good
Teacher Myth

Devils and Underdevils come to order!"

An unholy convocation of fallen angels commenced in the cavernous meeting room of Underearth.

"This session has been ordered by the Evil One himself to discuss and decide strategy that will prevent humans from turning to the Enemy. A suggestion has been offered by Toescum."

A hideous, wart-faced devil rose from the front row and turned to face the devilish assembly.

"My despised colleagues," Toescum began, "I propose that our darkstars assigned to the world's cults and 'isms' and organized religions put forth the idea that the Enemy's Son was a 'good teacher.'"

"Curse you, Toescum!" spewed an objector who had risen to his horny feet on Toescum's right. "You should be cannibalized by the Assembly for suggesting friendly treatment of the Enemy's Son!" Several demons around Toescum licked their crusted lips in anticipation.

"You imbecile," Toescum retorted. "This is no friendly treatment I propose." He straightened proudly. "My suggestion is truly diabolical."

Another devil stood.

"How can you call such a simple-minded idea 'diabolical'?"

"Because," he replied, "to label Him a 'good teacher' will effectively class Him with Moses, Zoroaster, Mohammed . . . it is to damn Him with faint praise."

A silence of realization descended on the crowd.

"Don't you see, you half-wits, if humans believe He is only a 'good teacher,' they can dismiss His Lordship, His Divinity."

"No," responded a devil called Spewbile. "They'll never fall for that! He Himself made it very clear who He is."

"Spewbile's right," said another. "Humans have the Book. They know that He said Himself, 'Before Abraham was, I AM.' They've read His words about the glory He shared with the Father before the world began."

"Yes, you fool," Spewbile added. "They know He claimed the power to read men's minds and hearts and to forgive sins. They have His words, 'I have come down from heaven.' They know that He claimed the power to raise Himself from the dead and that witnesses confirmed His resurrection. They're not so foolish as to think a mere man, a 'good teacher' could do those things!

"And," asserted Spewbile with finality, "they will recognize that if those things He claimed about Himself were *not* true, then He was not a 'good teacher'. . . . He was a liar or a lunatic!"

A murmur arose in the room. Some demons around Toescum again licked their lips and looked at him with hungry eyes, but he appeared confident.

"I must remind my contemptible comrades of the human tendency that allows us such frequent success. Mortals will often choose a lie even when they know the truth. As the Enemy's Son Himself said in one of His stories, 'If they do not listen to Moses and the Prophets, they will not be convinced even if someone rises from the dead.'"

Toescum's lips parted in a sneering smile as he sat down. The hungry demons surrounding him exchanged disappointed glances.

"Toescum's proposal," bellowed the chairman, "meets with the approval of the Demonic Council. The propagation of the 'Good Teacher Myth' is now an official strategy of Hell."

Workout

Increase your power to confront the Good Teacher Myth with this workout:

Match the following references with Jesus' claims about Himself.

A. Matthew 5:17   "I have authority to lay [my life] down and authority to take it up again"

B. Matthew 12:8   "I have told you everything ahead of time"

C. Matthew 24:30   "If a man keeps my word, he will never see death"

D. Mark 2:10   "The Son of Man [will come] on the clouds . . . with power and great glory"

E. Mark 13:23   "The Son of Man is Lord of the Sabbath"

F. Luke 12:9   "I am [the Messiah]"

G. Luke 22:70   "The Son gives life"

H. John 4:25–26   "He who disowns me before men will be disowned before the angels of God"

I. John 5:21   "I am the resurrection and the life. He who believes in me will live"

J. John 8:51   "The Son of Man has authority . . . to forgive sins."

K. John 10:18   "I have . . . come to fulfill the Law"

L. John 11:25   "You are right in saying I am [the Son of God]"

5
Partial Jesus

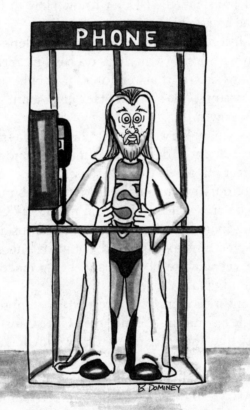

Exposing the Superstar
Myth

Andrew Lloyd Weber's rock opera *Jesus Christ Superstar* opened in the early 1970s to mixed reviews of "blasphemy!" and "inspirational!" In the play, Mary Magdalene sang a song about Jesus called, "I Don't Know How to Love Him," that became a radio hit.

In addition to portraying Mary Magdalene's romantic infatuation with Jesus (which has no basis in Scripture), the song contains a lyric that reinforces a popular myth about Christ. Mary sings, "He's a man / He's *just* a man."

That's a myth.

Jesus *is* a man. He was born as a human in a stable among cattle; the stench of dung and urine was among the first smells to greet His newly exposed senses.

But contrary to the Superstar Myth, that's not all He is. The Bible describes clearly the dual nature of "Christ Jesus: Who, being in very nature God, did not consider equality with God something to be grasped, but made himself nothing, taking the very nature of a servant, being made in human likeness" (Philippians 2:5–7).

For centuries men have wrestled to comprehend that duality of Jesus' nature. Sometimes Christians (and non-Christians, like the talented Andrew Lloyd Weber) have emphasized Jesus' humanity to the point that they have obscured His divinity. Others have made the opposite mistake. As a result, many people's understanding of Jesus Christ is partial. But the teaching of God's Word is clear. He is "God with us" (Matthew 1:23); yet He is also, in every respect, "the man Christ Jesus" (1 Timothy 2:5).

The classic *Arabian Nights* tells of the caliph of Baghdad's custom of walking the streets of the city while in disguise as a peasant so he could discover firsthand how his people lived. But Jesus did infinitely more than the caliph. He did not temporarily sacrifice royalty; He wrapped the rags of humanity around His divinity. "He came down to earth from Heaven who is God and Lord of all."

John, the disciple of Jesus, who walked dusty paths with Jesus, who shared earthy meals of lake bass and bread with Him, wrote of the one he knew as a man:

> In the beginning was the Word [Jesus], and the Word was with God, and the Word was God.
>
> *John 1:1*

And in that famous prologue to his Gospel, John leaves no doubt as to who he means when he refers to "the Word":

> The Word became flesh and made his dwelling among us. We have seen his glory, the glory of the One and Only, who came from the Father, full of grace and truth.
>
> *John 1:14*

Workout

Increase your power to confront the Superstar Myth with this workout:

Jesus and His disciples were Jews who held strong convictions about who was the appropriate object of men's worship. Read the following portions of Scripture and, in the space given, write who is the only proper object of worship, according to these verses:

Exodus 20:3 _____

Deuteronomy 6:14–15 _____

Luke 4:8 _____

Now read the following verses and indicate who, according to these Scripture verses, is the object of worship.

Matthew 2:2, 11 _____

Matthew 28:17 _____

Hebrews 1:6 _____

Since the Scriptures make it clear that only God is to be worshiped, can you draw any conclusions from the verses above about Jesus?

6
Pansy Jesus

Exposing the Meek and
Mild Myth

You are badly mistaken if you think that Jesus Christ was as weak, soft-spoken, or smooth-handed as some of our artists have made Him appear.

True, He was the Poet who spoke beautifully of the birds of the air and the lilies of the field. True, He was the folksy Storyteller who spun yarns of women baking bread and fishermen hauling in a catch. True, He was the gentle Nazarene who bounced little children on His lap and made them laugh. True, He was also the silent Prisoner who stood in perfect ease before kings and suffered bitter insults without uttering a word. But Jesus was nonetheless a man. A carpenter with calloused hands. An outdoorsman accustomed to long periods in the wilderness. A man who courageously spoke out against the corrupt authorities of His day, calling them "whitewashed tombs," "blind guides," and "serpents." As Bible scholar J. B. Phillips said:

> It is a thousand pities that the word "child" has so few words that rhyme with it appropriate for a hymn. [Otherwise] we might have been spared the couplet that hundreds of thousands must have learned in their childhood:
>
> > Gentle Jesus, meek and mild,
> > Look upon a little child.
>
> . . . This word "mild" is apparently deliberately used to describe a man who did not hesitate to challenge and expose the hypocrisies of the religious people of his day: a man who had such "personality" that He walked unscathed through a murderous crowd; a man so far from being a nonentity that He was regarded by authorities as a public danger . . . a man of such courage that He deliberately walked to what He knew

would mean death, despite the pleas of well-meaning friends!

The common perception of Jesus as soft, sentimental, and effeminate is a myth. He was gentle. He was meek. But that gentleness and meekness were not the absence of strength; it was *strength under control.*

According to the Gospels, Jesus stormed into the Temple in Jerusalem (perhaps on more than one occasion), to single-handedly drive out a large group of crooked merchants and moneychangers. *Not one* dared to protest or fight back against the red-hot blaze of His righteous indignation. More than that, although He had done something that would have been severely punished had any other man tried it, Jesus stayed there, not only to teach on the Temple steps but, as Mark relates, to prevent the moneychangers from returning. Jesus did not deal mildly with evil. He did not react gently to hypocrisy. He did not smile serenely on wickedness.

Sure, Jesus was a man who sat comfortably with children on His lap, but He was also a man who stood composed in the presence of His enemies.

Workout

Increase your power to confront the Meek and Mild Myth with this workout:

Read Luke 13:31–33. How does Jesus respond to the threat on His life? What word does He use to refer to Herod? Does this incident reveal anything about the strength of Jesus' character?

Read Matthew 23:1–39. Note the strength and severity of Jesus' words for the Pharisees and teachers of the Law. List the epithets He uses to describe them:

verse 13 _____

verse 16 _____

verse 17 _____

verse 19 _____

verse 33 _____

7

Plastic Jesus

Exposing the
Gumby Myth

L isten, man," Dan said as he shook a wrench in my face, "you can't tell me that some guy who lived two thousand years ago and spent most of His time walkin' around in a white robe tellin' stories to people is gonna make a difference to me today." He swept his arm around him to indicate the garage and the cars on blocks.

"I don't have time," he continued. "I mean, this Jesus stuff is okay for some people, like women and kids who may like the stories and maybe even get somethin' out of 'em . . . but for me? I don't think so. Jesus has nothin' to do with a guy that's got a timing chain to set on one car and a cracked engine block on the other."

Dan echoed the way a lot of people feel about Jesus. They see Him as a smiling, robed figure with a halo, like a plastic statue on a car dashboard. "Jesus is all right," they say, "for people with their heads in the clouds. But He really doesn't have much to do with people who are taking high school physics or who work in factories or whose kids need braces." Like Jesus has as much to do with real life in the modern world as Gumby and Pokey.

That's a myth.

Now, it's true that the founders of some non-Christian religions, like Buddhism and Confucianism, were men who lived lives of ease and contemplation.

But Jesus was a working man. He was a carpenter. I imagine Him in a shop that opens onto a dusty Nazareth street, with a sign over the door that reads, "Jesus ben Joseph, Carpenter." I picture Him bending over a cedar plank clamped to the bench in front of Him. He wears a leather apron; perspiration trickles down His face. He reaches for a knife, then a mallet. The shop is filled with the aromas of cedar and cypress from the shavings that cover the floor.

Jesus of Nazareth toiled as a carpenter for eighteen years or more. He developed muscles in His arms and calluses on His hands. He was acquainted with the demands of business: there were estimates to make, orders to take, prices to quote.

He knew the demands of family. Jesus had younger brothers and sisters who, upon the death of Joseph, became His responsibility. He undoubtedly knew what it was like to keep clothes on the kids and to try to get a fair price out of the merchants in the marketplace.

Jesus of Nazareth was no plastic saint. His world, like ours, was gritty, often smelly. His hands got dirty. He often slept on the ground. And when His life ended, He suffered a dirty, sweaty, bloody death. The great difference between Jesus' life and yours, though, is that His life and death brought forgiveness and salvation for "whoever believes in him" (John 3:16).

Workout

Increase your power to confront the Gumby Myth with this workout:

Read Mark 6:1–6. How did the people in Jesus' home-town of Nazareth know Him? As:

an ascetic

a contemplative

a saintly monk

a workman

Note also in this passage (and its parallel, Matthew 13:53–58) the reference to Jesus' brothers and sisters. Why would these siblings all have been younger than Jesus? Is there any other evidence in these verses that they were younger than Jesus and still at home in Nazareth?

8
Pink Jesus

Exposing the Racist Myth

Most Americans and Europeans picture Jesus of Nazareth looking something like Charlton Heston or Willem Defoe. Brown hair. Brown eyes. Handsome.

Oh yeah, He's also white. Caucasian. Suntanned, maybe, but definitely white. The kind of "white" that you might meet in California. Or Minneapolis. Or Peoria, Illinois.

But that's a myth.

Many people and movements have combined to perpetrate this myth. The Ku Klux Klan preaches the supremacy of white Protestants over blacks and Jews, among others. Some of them imagine that Jesus is on their side because He was white like them.

In the early days of Hitler's Nazi movement, Jesus' death was used to incite the masses against Jews. The Nazi "gospel" expounded white Aryan supremacy. They pretended that Jesus, of course, would be on their side. After all, He was "white," too, wasn't He?

The Crusades. The Inquisition. The pogroms of tsarist Russia. The importation of slaves to the New World. The Racist Myth has contributed to many of the most hideous crimes and cruelties in history.

The Racist Myth persists today. People still characterize Jesus as an Anglo-Saxon savior. They paint Him with pink and peach tones. They ascribe to Jesus the complexion, class, and customs of their Euro-American imaginations. But Jesus was neither white nor middle class.

In all probability, Jesus was much darker in complexion than the average American or European. He was born a Jew, He lived as a Jew, and He remained a Jew throughout His whole life. His swarthy Middle Eastern heritage was probably accentuated when He stood beside Pilate, a fair-skinned Roman.

But though Jesus entered the stage of humanity at a specific place and time and possessed specific racial characteristics (much less like Americans than Hollywood has ever conveyed), in a larger sense Jesus transcends barriers of race and color.

He was a Jew, yet He spoke freely and respectfully to a Samaritan woman.

As a Jew, custom prohibited Jesus from entering the home of a Gentile. Yet when a Roman centurion pleaded on behalf of his servant who lay sick at home, Jesus replied, "I will go and heal him."

When He was hounded by a Canaanite woman (Canaanites were historic enemies of the Jewish people), Jesus commended her faith and healed her daughter.

He was a victim of racial prejudice, too. On one trip through Samaria, He was rejected because the Samaritans guessed that He was a Jew bound for Jerusalem.

The society that Jesus entered when He became a man drew three primary distinctions among individuals. People's rights, privileges, and status were determined by their race (Jew or Gentile), class (slave or free), and sex (male or female). The good news that Jesus brought, however, presented a radical departure from the prejudices of the past. Paul encapsulized it eloquently when he wrote, "You are all sons of God through faith in Christ Jesus, for all of you who were baptized into Christ have clothed yourselves with Christ. There is neither Jew nor Greek, slave nor free, male nor female, for you are all one in Christ Jesus" (Galatians 3:26–28).

The followers of Jesus must be like Him, not in pigmentation or racial characteristics, but in accepting and loving people regardless of sex, class, or race distinctions.

Some children see Him lily white,
The Baby Jesus born this night.
Some children see Him lily white,
With tresses soft and fair.

Some children see Him bronzed and brown,
The Lord of heav'n to earth come down.
Some children see Him bronzed and brown,
With dark and heavy hair.

Some children see Him almond-eyed,
This Savior whom we kneel beside.
Some children see Him almond-eyed,
With skin of yellow hue.

Some children see Him dark as they,
Sweet Mary's Son to whom we pray.
Some children see Him dark as they,
And, ah! they love Him too!

The children in each diff'rent place
Will see the Baby Jesus' face
Like theirs, but bright with heav'nly grace,
And filled with holy light.

O lay aside each earthly thing,
And with thy heart as offering,
Come worship now the Infant King.
'Tis love that's born tonight.

Workout

Increase your power to confront the Racist Myth with this workout:

The following verses refer to incidents cited or verses quoted in this chapter. Read each passage, jot down an identifying phrase in the space provided, and label the paragraphs above with the number of the reference below.

1. Luke 9:51–56 _____

2. John 4:1–26 _____

3. Galatians 3:26–28 _____

4. Matthew 8:5–13 _____

5. Matthew 15:21–28 _____

Myths About the Bible

9
The One, The Only

Exposing the Just Another
Great Book Myth

You've heard it. Probably not just once, either. In that tone of voice people use when talking to mental patients:

"Oh, you don't read the Bible, do you?"

At other times, a person will pat you like you're an obedient puppy and say, "Yeah, the Bible's okay. It's sure a lot better than that *Iliad* and *Odyssey* stuff."

And, of course, occasionally you'll run into the teacher or professor who boasts of having the King James Version nestled on a shelf—dusty maybe, not broken in, but there nonetheless—alongside Plato's *Republic*, Virgil's *Aeneid*, and Shakespeare's Complete Works, in its rightful place as one of the "great" works of literature.

That's a myth.

The Bible is not one of many great books. It is the one. The only.

If your English teachers want to place it on a shelf with others in its class, you'd better tell them that they need to buy a whole new bookcase. And the Bible needs to be on the top shelf. By itself.

The Bible is unique.

In *All About the Bible*, Sidney Collett cites Professor M. Montiero-Williams, who spent forty-two years studying Eastern books. He said, "Pile them, if you will, on the left side of your study table; but place your own Holy Bible on the right side—all by itself, all alone—and with a wide gap between them. For . . . there is a gulf between it and the so-called sacred books of the East which severs the one from the other utterly, hopelessly, and forever . . . a veritable gulf which cannot be bridged."

The Bible is a miracle of literary accomplishment. Some books take a lifetime to write; the Bible was composed over a period of roughly sixteen hundred years. Some books require the collaboration of a team of scholars; the Bible is the work of more than forty authors from every walk of life, including kings, peasants, philosophers, fishermen, poets, statesmen, and scholars. Portions of the Bible were written in the wilderness, in a dungeon, in a palace, in exile, in wartime, and in peacetime.

The Bible was written on three continents in three languages on hundreds of controversial subjects. It contains flashes of inspired poetry as well as detailed history, captivating biography, letters, memoirs, and prophetic writings. Yet this astoundingly diverse book speaks with astonishing continuity. There is one unfolding story from page one to "The End"—God's redemption of man.

A representative of the *Great Books of the Western World* came to my house one day recruiting salesmen for that series. He spent five minutes talking to me about the Great Books series, after which I spent ninety minutes talking to him about the Greatest Book.

I challenged him to take just ten of the authors in the Great Books series, all from one walk of life, one generation, one place, one time, one mood, one continent, one language, and one controversial subject.

Then I asked, "Would those authors agree?"

The man paused and answered, "No."

"What would you have?" I asked.

Immediately he said, "A conglomeration!"

Two days later, that man committed his life to Christ because he recognized the uniqueness of the Bible and its message.

Workout

Increase your power to confront the Just Another Great Book Myth by reading each reference below in which the

Bible likens itself to some other object that is mighty in influence. Read each reference carefully. Then list what the Bible parallels, and consider why—in what way(s)—the Bible is like that object. Also ponder whether there is any other book of which such things could be claimed.

Jeremiah 5:14 _____

Jeremiah 23:29 _____

Romans 1:16 _____

Ephesians 6:17 _____

Hebrews 4:12 _____

10
The Bible and Swiss Cheese

Exposing the
Holey Bible Myth

Many people, whether they realize it or not, regard the Bible much like swiss cheese: There's a lot of good stuff there, but it's got a lot of holes in it, too.

"Oh, the Bible is helpful and inspirational," they'll say. "I especially love the Psalms, like, Psalm 23 is soo beeeautiful."

But if you press them far enough, they'll eventually admit, "Of course, there are problems in the Bible, y'know? I mean, mistakes and all. But that doesn't bother me. After all, it wasn't written to be a history textbook. It's accurate where it needs to be, like in matters of faith and doctrine."

That's a myth.

Very often, the people who make such statements have only vague ideas as to what "mistakes" they're talking about. The Bible is not full of holes. It is not riddled with mistakes. It is the inspired Word of God, remarkably written over a period of about sixteen hundred years by about forty different authors. It has been remarkably preserved from the original manuscripts by painstaking copyists and careful scholars. The Old and New Testaments are *the* most accurately preserved and widely attested documents of the ancient world.

The followers of Jesus cannot ignore the fact that the Lord Himself believed in the accuracy of the Scriptures. He said, "the Scripture cannot be broken" (John 10:35). He related the experience of Jonah as fact. He quoted Scripture in His desert battle with Satan. He referred repeatedly to the Scriptures in His teaching. He regarded the teachings, historical details, and events of the Old Testament as accurate.

The New Testament writers likewise confirmed the reliability of all Scripture. The Apostle Paul wrote, "All Scripture is God-breathed and is useful for teaching, rebuking, correcting and training in righteousness" (2 Timothy

3:16). And he, with the other apostles, acknowledged the inspiration of the New Testament writings with such statements as: "what I am writing to you is the Lord's command" (1 Corinthians 14:37).

There do occur in the Bible different perspectives of the same event, different emphases in retelling incidents and other *apparent* discrepancies. There have been difficulties in translating the original Hebrew or Greek text. There have been a host of misinterpretations of biblical passages. Nonetheless, when twentieth-century Christians open the Bible, they are reading the inspired, preserved, reliable Word of God. "The grass withers," said Isaiah, "and the flowers fall, but the word of our God stands forever" (Isaiah 40:8).

Workout

Increase your power to confront the Holey Bible Myth with this workout:

Read Matthew 4:1–11. Jesus answers each temptation of the devil with a reference to Scripture. Using a concordance or a reference Bible, determine the Scripture He quotes, then write the reference below:

verse 4 _____

verse 7 _____

verse 10 _____

Read the following:

Matthew 12:38–41, in which Jesus refers to the prophet's experience recorded in the Book of Jonah.

Mark 2:23–26, in which Jesus refers to an incident recorded in 1 Samuel 21:6–7.

John 3:14–15, in which Jesus refers to an event detailed in Numbers 21.

Now evaluate: Does Jesus express any doubt or misgivings about the factuality of these people, events, and accounts, or does He seem to accept them as reliable? Does that provide any guidance for you?

11

The Bible and the Telephone Game

AND THIS IS WHAT
GOD SAYS FOR
US TO WRITE ...

B. DOMINEY

Exposing the Variant
Readings Myth

The telephone game has not only been a popular group game for years, but it has also been used to illustrate the value of accuracy in communication.

In the game, a group of people sit in a circle. One person whispers a brief message to the person next to him. That person repeats the phrase to the next person, and so on until the message is whispered around the circle.

Often the words that return to the person who started the message on its circular journey are different—often comically so. A message that started out as "If you don't use your muscles, they'll usually become stiff" may end up as "Choosy mothers choose Jif!"

Many people believe that something like the telephone game has happened in the case of the Bible—you know, that what you have between two leather covers (with your name printed in gold on the front) is so far removed from what was *really* written thousands of years ago that no one can believe in it very much.

That's a myth.

First of all, the Old Testament was copied with such precision that, when an entire scroll had been copied by hand, one letter at a time, if one mistake was made, the scroll was destroyed.

In addition, the Jewish copyists of the Hebrew Scriptures adhered to detailed requirements in copying:

• each copy had to be made on a brand new writing surface and had to be prepared in a specific way;

• each copy had to be written in a certain number of columns of thirty-letters width, with a certain number of lines to each column;

- each copy had to be written in a certain color and quality of ink;

- each copy had to be made from an authenticated original;

- not even the tiniest letter could be written from memory, as one would glance at the word "to" and write the letters "t" and "o" before glancing back at the original, but *every* letter was copied singly from the original;

- no letter could connect with or overlap another letter. The distance between each letter was measured by a single hair or thread;

- every letter of every page and book was counted and compared against the original. The number of times each letter of the alphabet occurred in a book was counted and compared against the original. The middle letter of the Pentateuch (the first five books of the Old Testament) and the middle letter of the entire Hebrew Bible were computed and indicated in the text. If *one* of these calculations was incorrect, the copy was discarded.

And that's just the Old Testament. The New Testament is unquestionably *the* most reliable, attested document of the ancient world.

When you study Plato in school, does the teacher express skepticism about the reliability of *Republic?*

When your ancient history teacher has you read aloud from the poetry of Catullus or Julius Caesar's account of *The Gallic Wars,* does she warn you that what you're reading may be unreliable?

Do your instructors dismiss the writings of the Greek historian Thucydides or the philosopher Aristotle or the tragedians Sophocles and Euripides as being unworthy of serious consideration because of textual problems and variant readings?

Probably not. Yet many people think the Bible is a faulty document, when in fact none of those other works can approach the reliability of the New Testament text.

Two factors are most important in determining the reliability of a historical document: the number of manuscript copies in existence, and the time between when it was first written and the oldest existing copy.

When you compare the New Testament with other ancient writer's works, its reliability is immediately obvious.

Author	Written	Earliest Copies	Time Span	No. of Copies
Caesar	100–44 B.C.	A.D. 900	1,000 yrs.	10
Plato (*Tetralogies*)	427–347 B.C.	A.D. 900	1,200 yrs.	7
Thucydides	460–400 B.C.	A.D. 900	1,300 yrs.	8
Sophocles	496–406 B.C.	A.D. 1,000	1,400 yrs.	100
Catullus	54 B.C.	A.D. 1,550	1,600 yrs.	3
Euripides	480–406 B.C.	A.D. 1,100	1,500 yrs.	9
Aristotle	384–322 B.C.	A.D. 1,100	1,400 yrs.	5

Compare the New Testament to those writers of antiquity:

Author	Written	Earliest Copies	Time Span	No. of Copies
New Testament	A.D. 40–100	A.D. 125	25 yrs.	24,000+

No other ancient document even comes close. The runner-up for textual reliability is Homer's *Iliad*, with 643 manuscript copies and a five-hundred-year span between the time it was written and the oldest existing copy.

Is the Bible reliable? Compared to any other work of antiquity, it can be said of the Bible—"It's in a league all by itself."

Workout

Increase your power to confront the Variant Readings Myth with this workout:

Fill in the missing words in the following verses:

"Your word, O Lord, is _____." (Psalm 119:89)

"Long ago I learned from your statutes that you established them _____ _____ _____." (Psalm 119:152)

"The grass _____ and the flowers _____, but the word of our God _____ _____." (Isaiah 40:8)

"I tell you the truth, until heaven and earth disappear, not the smallest _____, not the least _____ _____ _____ will by any means disappear from the Law until everything is accomplished." (Matthew 5:18)

Do any of the above verses apply to the Variant Readings Myth? If they do, in what way?

12
Changing Fact to Fiction

Exposing the Myths and
Legends Myth

Annie met a tidal wave of reaction when she proposed that the Bible be included on a reading list for a college course on world literature.

"You can't be serious!" someone said. "The Bible?"

Another responded, "You can't tell me that you believe in that Jonah-and-the-whale stuff! And walking on water? C'mon, get real!"

"Let's be reasonable," came another response. "The Bible may have its place in religion, but that's where it belongs. It has some fascinating myths and legends, I'll grant you that, but don't ask me to take it seriously."

In recent years, some people have come to think that way. Even some Bible scholars have decided that the Bible is best understood as a compilation of religious folklore and legends. In other words, they're trying to change fact to fiction.

Admittedly, the Bible does tell some pretty extraordinary stories, some of which sound more like headlines from supermarket tabloids than historical records:

MAN WALKS ON WATER

LITTLE BOY'S LUNCHBOX FEEDS THOUSANDS,

CHANGE WATER TO WINE IN ONE EASY STEP

GALILEAN TEACHER RETURNS FROM THE GRAVE

No matter how incredible some Bible stories may *seem*, however, the people who reported these things clearly intended their accounts to be understood not as myth or legend, but as fact.

Not only that, but the New Testament writers knew that relating such remarkable facts might cost them their lives.

How many people do *you* know who would gladly be imprisoned, even executed, for refusing to recant a legend?

In addition, certainly the New Testament writers knew that telling stories about a rabbi raising himself from the dead or five thousand people being fed from five loaves and two fish is a sure ticket to the funny farm—unless there were other witnesses.

That's why the Apostle Paul, for example, proclaimed the truth of the Gospel before a king named Agrippa and a Roman governor named Festus. When Paul spoke of the resurrection of Christ, the Bible reports:

> At this point Festus interrupted Paul's defense. "You are out of your mind, Paul!" he shouted. "Your great learning is driving you insane."
>
> "I am not insane, most excellent Festus," Paul replied. "What I am saying is true and reasonable. The king is familiar with these things, and I can speak freely to him. I am convinced that none of this has escaped his notice, because *it was not done in a corner.*"
>
> *Acts 26:24–26 (emphasis added)*

Contrary to the myths, legends, and mystery religions of the ancient world, the events recorded in the Bible were "not done in a corner." A whole bunch of people saw them as they happened. Reliable people testified—in writing—to the authenticity of those events and signed their testimony in blood. And those writings, far from being effectively refuted and discredited, stood the test and were recognized as authoritative.

Peter himself answered the Myths and Legends Myth when he wrote, "We did not follow cleverly invented stories when we told you about the power and coming of our Lord Jesus Christ, but we were eyewitnesses of his majesty" (2 Peter 1:16).

Workout

Increase your power to confront the Myths and Legends Myth with this workout:

Read Luke 1:1–3. Who is writing these words? Who told the author about "the things accomplished among us?" What did the author do *before* writing his account for Theophilus?

Read 1 John 1:3. Who is writing these words? Does he claim to be an eyewitness? What is his purpose in relating what he has seen and heard?

Read Acts 2:22. Who is speaking these words? To whom were they spoken? What is the significance of the speaker's words, "as you yourselves know"?

Read John 19:35. Who is the writer? Was he an eyewitness to the things he wrote about? Does he intend what he wrote to be understood as fact or fiction? Notice that he wrote "so that you also may believe." Take a moment to prayerfully reflect on the witness of the New Testament writers and determine whether John's purpose has been achieved in you.

13

Dr. Luke and the Case of the Disappearing Politarch

Exposing the Archaeological Myth

The stout man ascended the steps of 221B Baker Street and was ushered into the presence of the great detective.

"Ah, good morning, Doctor!" said the lean figure in the armchair. "I see you've had some sleepless nights lately."

"Yes, I'm afraid—wait a minute. How do you know that? And how can you know I'm a doctor?"

"Oh, elementary, I'm afraid. You're also quite a writer, I see, and have come quite a distance. But never mind all that. Tell me about your recent trouble."

The visitor struggled to overcome his confusion and finally managed to begin an explanation.

"I'm Dr. Luke," he explained, "author of two bestselling books—about events of my day, the first Christian century."

The detective, Sherlock Holmes, tented his fingertips in front of him and listened.

"Lately," Dr. Luke continued, "my reputation has been shattered. My intelligence and character have been called into question.

"You see, in my Book of Acts, I referred to the city of Iconium as being outside a district called Lycaonia. Some archaeologists, based on some other writings, concluded that Iconium was a Lycaonian city and pronounced my book unreliable.

"Not only that," Luke went on, afraid that Holmes would think he was just being sensitive, "but in my Gospel account I referred to a man named Lysanias, the tetrarch of Abilene, at the beginning of John the Baptist's ministry in A.D. 27. Again, I was accused of sloppy work because archaeologists knew of only one Lysanias, and he was killed in 36 B.C. "And I used the word *proconsul* to refer to Gallio in my account of Paul's ministry in Corinth—the 'scholars' said I didn't know what I was talking about—that *proconsul* would never have been used to refer to a man in Gallio's position!

"Most maddening of all, perhaps, is the abuse I've taken from so-called scholars for using the Greek word *politarchs* to refer to the city officials at Thessalonica. Since that word is found nowhere else in classical literature, the archaeologists and critics are all pointing to that, saying, 'Luke is wrong; you can't believe what he writes, na-na-na-na-na-na.' And there are more, even tinier points with which they've tried to discredit me."

Holmes's eyes were closed and his breathing slow when Dr. Luke finished his narrative. Finally, he opened his eyes and stood with an air of finality.

"I'm sorry, Doctor," he said, "but I can do nothing for you."

The physician stood and stared wordlessly at the famous detective.

"Am I right in assuming, Doctor," Holmes asked, "that you're certain of the accuracy of the history you've recorded?"

"Absolutely!" Dr. Luke said, straightening himself to his full height. "I am a historian, sir!"

"Then you must wait," he said, guiding the great historian to the door. "There will come a day when your careful record will be vindicated on each of those points. Until then," he said, before he closed the door on the exasperated physician, "my good doctor, you must wait, secure in the knowledge that when vindication does come, you will have been right all along."

That encounter between the first-century historian and the fictional detective never happened, of course. But everything Luke says in the above account is true. He has been much maligned in years past. But if Holmes had offered such advice to Dr. Luke, it would have been 100 percent correct.

Although scholars and archaeologists have repeatedly attacked Luke for inaccuracies and misstatements, he has been vindicated repeatedly—by archaeology.

Many people entertain the idea that the modern science of archaeology has "proven" the Bible wrong in places. But the opposite is true. Take Luke's first complaint, for example. In 1910, archaeologist Sir William Ramsay found a monument that showed that Iconium was a *Phrygian* city. Later discoveries, too, confirmed Luke's account.

An archaeological find near Damascus confirmed the existence of a "Lysanias the Tetrarch" and is dated between A.D. 14 and 29, perfectly supporting Luke's record.

Luke's reference to Gallio has been vindicated by an inscription that states, in part, "As Lucius Junius Gallio, my friend, and the Proconsul of Achaia . . ."

And the disappearing politarch, which was once considered conclusive evidence of Luke's unreliability, has since reappeared. In recent years, more than a dozen inscriptions have been unearthed which make use of that ancient Greek title.

The idea that archaeology has disproved the Bible is not only outdated—it's a myth. As archaeologist William F. Albright has said,

> The excessive skepticism shown toward the Bible by important historical schools of the eighteenth and nineteenth centuries, certain phases of which still appear periodically, has been progressively discredited. Discovery after discovery has established the accuracy of innumerable details, and has brought increased recognition to the value of the Bible as a source of history.

In other words, Sherlock was right.

Workout

Increase your power to confront the Archaeological Myth by reading the following portions of Scripture and filling in the name of the individual whose existence and identity, long stated in the Bible, has been supported by recent archaeological discovery:

Daniel 5:30   Once thought to be an embarrassing mistake (since a clay tablet named Nabonidus as the last king of Babylon), later research supported the existence of _____, the son of Nabonidus, who ruled as co-regent with his father.

Romans 16:23   Excavations in 1929 revealed a man known as _____ and identified him as the director of public works in Corinth.

Matthew 27:1–2   A 1961 discovery in the Mediterranean port of Caesarea uncovered a 2' x 3' inscription referring to _____.

14

Truth or Coincidences?

Exposing the Coincidence Myth

Nathan burst through the kitchen door and nearly plowed his mother off her feet.

"Nathan!" she snapped.

"Sorry, Mom," he said, "but you've gotta see this book I got from Todd." He spilled his schoolbooks onto the counter and lifted one out of the pile. "It's a bunch of predictions and stuff by some old guy named Nostril something or other."

"Nostradamus?"

"Yeah, that's it!" Nathan answered. "You've heard of him?"

"Mm hmm," she said.

"Isn't he wild? He predicted all sorts of things before they happened, like Hitler and World War II, and Kennedy's assassination. Todd said there's even something in here about M. C. Hammer."

"That's what Todd said, huh?"

Nathan paused and searched his mom's face suspiciously. "Okay, Mom, what's up? You've got that look again."

"Oh, nothing, really. I just wonder—did you *see* those 'prophecies' he made? I mean, did you look them up, or did someone show them to you, or what?"

"Yeah, well, Todd pointed them out to me."

"Didn't they seem kind of vague? Like they might apply to any number of situations or interpretations?"

Nathan thought, then shrugged. "I guess."

"It's amazing to me that people get so wrapped up in Nostradamus's doubtful prophecies and so completely ignore the divinely inspired and clearly fulfilled prophecies of Scripture!"

Nathan was interested. He put the Nostradamus book down. "Like what?"

"Like what?" she echoed. "Nathan, I'm surprised at you. Like Jesus being born in Bethlehem. Micah predicted that. And Zechariah predicted that the Messiah would ride into Jerusalem, not on a mighty war horse, but on a donkey."

"Oh yeah," Nathan said. "And that He would be betrayed, too, right?"

"Right. Betrayed by a friend, for thirty pieces of silver, that His hands and feet would be pierced, that His bones would not be broken—*details*, Nathan, not vague generalizations or lucky guesses, but dozens of specific predictions that came true with 100 percent accuracy. And that's just the Messianic prophecies. The same is true of prophecies about cities and nations all through the Bible."

"Makes Nostradamus look sick, doesn't it?" Nathan concluded.

"Dead in the water," his mom said with a smile.

Nathan's mom is right. Biblical prophecy reveals with startling force the unique character and reliability of the Hebrew and Christian Scriptures.

Even a casual awareness of the prophecies concerning the Messiah must convince all but the most biased reader of the truth of the Bible.

But some imaginative people think that the fulfillment of biblical prophecy is due to coincidence. "You could find some of those prophecies fulfilled in President Kennedy or Martin Luther King," some have said.

Yes, but could you find *all* of the *forty-eight major prophecies* concerning the Messiah fulfilled in any one man? In a word, "Nope."

The chances of that happening by coincidence, says Peter Stoner in *Science Speaks*, is 1 in 10 to the power of 157, or the number 10 followed by 157 zeroes. You can't imagine a number that big or a probability that small.

Such astronomical odds make it clear that the prophecies

of the Bible were not lucky guesses, "For prophecy never had its origin in the will of man," as Peter said, "but men spoke from God as they were carried along by the Holy Spirit" (2 Peter 1:21).

Work Out

Increase your power to confront the Coincidence Myth by seeing how many of the following you can correctly match with the prophet who predicted it or the book in which it's found. The answers are:

A. Genesis   C. Isaiah   E. Micah
B. Psalms   D. Jeremiah   F. Zechariah

The questions are:

1. Jesus would be born of a virgin (Matthew 1:18–25)
2. Of the tribe of Judah (Luke 3:23, 33)
3. Descended from Jesse (Luke 3:32)
4. Of the house of David (Luke 3:31)
5. Born in Bethlehem (Matthew 2:1)
6. Preceded by a messenger (Matthew 3:1–2)
7. Enter Jerusalem on a donkey (Luke 19:35–37)
8. Betrayed by a friend (Matthew 26:48–50)
9. Betrayed for thirty pieces of silver (Matthew 26:15)
10. Silent before His accusers (Matthew 27:12)
11. Hands and feet pierced (Luke 23:33; John 20:25)
12. Crucified with thieves (Matthew 27:38)
13. Interceded for His persecutors (Luke 23:34)
14. Garments parted (John 19:23)

15. Lots cast for garments (John 19:24)
16. Gall and vinegar offered to Him (Matthew 27:34)
17. His bones not broken (John 19:33)
18. His side pierced (John 19:34)
19. He was buried with the rich (Matthew 27:57–60)
20. His resurrection (Acts 2:31).

Answers: 1. C (Isaiah 7:14) 2. A (Genesis 49:10) 3. C (Isaiah 11:1) 4. D (Jeremiah 23:5) 5. E (Micah 5:2) 6. C (Isaiah 40:3) 7. F (Zechariah 9:9) 8. B (Psalm 41:9) 9. F (Zechariah 11:12) 10. C (Isaiah 53:7) 11. B (Psalm 22:16) 12. C (Isaiah 53:12) 13. C (Isaiah 53:12) 14. B (Psalm 22:18) 15. B (Psalm 22:18) 16. B (Psalm 69:21) 17. B (Psalm 34:20) 18. F (Zechariah 12:10) 19. C (Isaiah 53:9) 20. B (Psalm 16:10).

Myths About the Resurrection

15
Playing Dead?

Exposing the Swoon Myth

I set out as a young man to refute Christianity and prove it to be a joke. That didn't happen, of course, for a very simple reason: I am unable to explain away an event in history—the resurrection of Jesus Christ.

The resurrection is central to Christianity. As Michael Green has said in his book, *Man Alive*, "Christianity does not hold the resurrection to be one among many tenets of belief. Without faith in the resurrection there would be no Christianity at all. The Christian church would never have begun; the Jesus movement would have fizzled out like a damp squib with his execution. Christianity stands or falls with the truth of the resurrection. Once you disprove it, and you have disposed of Christianity."

That, certainly, is why so many people have attacked the resurrection and set out to disprove it.

Dr. Hugh Schonfield's book, *The Passover Plot*, caused a volcanic controversy upon its appearance in the mid-1960s. Schonfield's book caused such a fuss because it argued an old explanation for the resurrection of Jesus Christ that has been called the Swoon Theory.

The swoon theory was made popular by a man named Venturini several centuries ago, and it supposes that Jesus didn't really die. He merely fainted (or "swooned") from exhaustion and loss of blood. Everyone thought Him to be dead, so the theory goes, but He later recovered and the disciples thought He rose from the dead.

Schonfield played a clever variation of the swoon theory, concluding that Jesus planned His arrest, trial, and crucifixion, arranging for Himself to be drugged on the cross so that He could feign death and recover from the beatings, exposure, trauma, and loss of blood from the spear wound in His side and the bloody holes in His hands and feet where spikes that supported His weight on the cross had ripped His flesh and bones.

But the swoon theory is a myth.

Jesus had undergone a vicious beating with an instrument known as a flagrum, which cut and ripped the victim to shreds. Prisoners occasionally missed their own execution because they could not survive the scourging.

Then, after bearing intense punishment, Jesus underwent the journey to the place of death. But He had suffered so much He could not complete the journey—Matthew and Luke relate that Simon of Cyrene was forced to carry the cross after Jesus collapsed. Mark's statement that "they brought Jesus to the place called Golgotha" (Mark 15:22) may indicate that He was unable even to walk under His own power.

Jesus then experienced a means of death that defies description, although Frederick Farrar offers a complete attempt:

> Death by crucifixion seems to include all that pain and death *can* have of horrible and ghastly—dizziness, cramp, thirst, starvation, sleeplessness, traumatic fever, tetanus, shame, publicity of shame, long continuance of torment, horror of anticipation, mortification of untended wounds—all intensified just up to the point at which they can be endured at all, but all stopping just short of the point which would give to the sufferer the relief of unconsciousness.
>
> The unnatural position made every movement painful; the lacerated veins and crushed tendons throbbed with incessant anguish; the wounds, inflamed by exposure, gradually gangrened; the arteries—especially at the head and stomach—became swollen and oppressed with surcharged blood; and while each variety

of misery went on gradually increasing, there was added to them the intolerable pang of a burning and raging thirst; and all these physical complications caused an internal excitement and anxiety, which made the prospect of death itself—of death, the unknown enemy, at whose approach man usually shudders most—bear the aspect of delicious and exquisite release.

Following hours of such treatment, Jesus was removed from the cross—but only after a Roman centurion (who certainly knew death when he saw it) had certified to the Roman governor that Jesus of Nazareth was dead.

To imagine that a man survived that experience and emerged from it to appear in Judea and Galilee to more than five hundred people as the Conqueror of Death and Prince of Life must certainly require a huge willingness to rewrite history and ignore the simple truth: "that Christ died for our sins according to the Scriptures, that he was buried, that he was raised on the third day according to the Scriptures" (1 Corinthians 15:3–4).

Workout

Increase your power to confront the Swoon Myth with this workout:

Read John 19:30–35. Why did the soldiers not break Jesus' legs? How many Roman soldiers (at least) knew Jesus to be dead? Who is "the man" mentioned in verse 35? What does he know to be true?

Read Mark 15:42–47. How many *eyewitnesses* of Jesus' death are mentioned in these verses?

Read Matthew 27:62–66. Were the chief priests and Pharisees convinced that Jesus was dead? Note verse 3— since they were aware of Jesus' promise to rise again, is it likely they would have allowed a live Jesus to be taken from the cross?

Of those mentioned above, how many unsympathetic witnesses knew of Jesus' death (that is, how many not counting Jesus' followers and friends)?

16
Blind Man's Bluff?

Exposing the Wrong
Tomb Myth

I don't mind tellin' you, Lizzie, it was the strangest thing! It was me and the other Mary and uh, let's see, oh yeah, Salome and, and . . . give me a minute, I'll remember—"

"Will you get on with it?" Elizabeth urged.

"Who's doin' the talking here? I'm getting on with it, I'm getting on with it. Anyhow, we went to the tomb just after sunrise, it was still not quite light out, you know how it gets, you gotta watch out for clotheslines and cobwebs and—"

Elizabeth rolled her eyes in exasperation.

"All right, all right," Mary said. "As I was saying, we went and found an empty tomb where just the night before we had laid Jesus. Did you hear what I said, Lizzie? It was empty! Nothing there. NUHthing!"

Elizabeth stared at her friend. "Are you sure it was the right tomb?"

"Am I sure it was—land sakes, Lizzie! What kind of question is that? Am I sure it was the right tomb? Give me a little credit, will you? It's not like I was the only one there . . . we went together, and Mary and I had been there just the night before. If we were at the wrong tomb don't you think *one* of us might have figured that out? How stupid do you think we are?"

"And if you think we were lost, what about the angels? I didn't even tell you about the angels, did I? Yeah, well they were at the empty tomb, too, shining like lightning! They told us not to be afraid, Jesus was risen, just as He had said. I suppose you think the angels showed up at the wrong tomb, too, eh?"

"I didn't mean anything by it, I just—"

"And while you're calling me stupid, you might as well call Peter and John baboons! After all, I ran to tell them, and they ran *straight* to the empty tomb! They beat me back there!"

"And what's more, Miss Are-You-Sure-It-Was-the-Right-Tomb, how many tombs in Jerusalem do you think had the remnants of a broken Roman seal?"

"Well, I, I—"

"And what about the chief priests and the guard? Don't you think they knew which tomb was the right one? If we went to the wrong tomb, wouldn't they just have to go to the right one and say, 'Ha! Proved you wrong! Here's the body!' Huh? Huh?"

Elizabeth threw up her hands. "I'm sorry, OK? I didn't mean to suggest anything so stupid."

Unfortunately, Elizabeth isn't the only one to make such a suggestion. Kirsopp Lake theorized that the women who reported the missing body of Jesus actually went to the wrong tomb. But, as Mary so adamantly suggested to Elizabeth, a fifteen-minute walk from the palace of the high priest or the Roman fortress in Jerusalem could have effectively—and quickly—quenched for all time any rumor of a resurrection.

But that didn't happen, of course. Because it really was Jesus' tomb the women found. And they found it empty.

Workout

Increase your power to confront the Wrong Tomb Myth with this workout:

Read Matthew 27:57–28:15. List the individuals or groups of people who would have known the correct location of the tomb:

Matthew 27:59–60 _____

Matthew 27:61 _____ and _____

Matthew 27:62–66 _____

Matthew 28:2–4, 11 _____

John mentions someone else who would have known the location of Jesus' burial place (John 19:38–41). Who?

Notice that Matthew, Mark, and Luke all mention that the women *saw* Jesus' burial (Matthew 27:61; Mark 15:47; Luke 23:55). Why did they all record that?

17
Hide 'n' Seek?

Exposing the Stolen Body
Myth

The Bible itself contains the first mention of the Stolen Body Myth. After the Resurrection, some of the soldiers who had been guarding the tomb went to the chief priests and reported what had happened. Matthew reports:

> When the chief priests had met with the elders and devised a plan, they gave the soldiers a large sum of money, telling them, "You are to say, 'His disciples came during the night and stole him away while we were asleep.' If this report gets to the governor, we will satisfy him and keep you out of trouble." So the soldiers took the money and did as they were instructed. And this story has been widely circulated among the Jews to this very day.
>
> *Matthew 28:12–15*

In spite of the fact that the New Testament itself relates the origin of the Stolen Body Myth, some people today still imagine that the disciples played a little game of hide 'n' seek with Jesus' body.

However, many factors make such a story impossible to believe. The stone, for example, that sealed the tomb after Jesus was buried was not the kind of stone people skim across the surface of a lake. According to textual information and the calculations of two Georgia Tech engineering professors, it may well have been a five-foot-high circular stone weighing around two tons. When the tomb was first prepared, a team of laborers probably would have set the stone in place with a wedge as it sat in a trench that sloped down to the front of the tomb. When Jesus was buried, the wedge was removed and gravity did the rest, sealing the tomb in such a way that it could only be reopened with much noisy heaving by a team of

strong men. That's why the women, on their way to the tomb
Easter Sunday morning, wondered, "Who will roll the stone
away from the entrance of the tomb?" (Mark 16:3).

Furthermore, the chief priests acted to prevent the theft
of the body, requesting a detachment of soldiers from Pilate,
the Roman governor. A Roman guard unit was a four- to six-
teen-man security force. Each man was trained to protect six
feet of ground. Sixteen men were placed in a square forma-
tion, with four on each side. They were supposed to be able
to protect thirty-six yards against an entire battalion and
hold it.

Normally, four men were placed immediately in front of
what they were to protect. The other twelve slept in a semi-
circle in front of them with their heads pointing in. To steal
what these guards were protecting, thieves would first have to
walk over those who were asleep (in full view, of course, of
the others who were awake). Every four hours, another unit of
four was awakened, and those who had been awake took a
turn at sleeping. They would rotate this way around the
clock.

These men were not polite tour guides, either. They
were dangerous fighting machines. T. G. Tucker, in his book,
Life in the Roman World of Nero and St. Paul, describes one of
these soldiers:

> Over his breast, and with flaps over the shoulders, he
> will wear a corset of leather covered with hoop-like lay-
> ers, or maybe scales, of iron or bronze. On his head will
> be a plain pot-like helmet, or skull-cap, of iron.
>
> In his right hand he will carry the famous Roman
> pike. This is a stout weapon, over 6 feet in length, con-
> sisting of a sharp iron head fixed on a wooden shaft, and
> the soldier may either charge with it as a bayonet, or he
> may hurl it like a javelin and then fight at close quarters
> with his sword.

> On the left arm is a shield . . . [which] is not only
> carried by means of a handle, but may be supported by a
> belt over the right shoulder. In order to be out of the way
> of the shield, the sword—a thrusting rather than a slash-
> ing weapon, approaching 3 feet in length—is hung at
> the right side by a belt passing over the left shoulder. . . .
> On the left side, the soldier wears a dagger.

Those who entertain the Stolen Body Myth suppose that
a group of disciples, who days before had run like scared
bunny rabbits, confronted a guard of heavily armed, battle-
trained Roman soldiers. They either overpowered them or
snuck past them in their sleep to move a two-ton stone up an
incline without waking a single man. Then, so the thinking
goes, the disciples carted off Jesus' body, hid it somewhere
and, over the course of the next several decades, endured
ridicule, torture, and martyrdom to spread a lie—what *they
knew to be a lie*—throughout the known world.

On the contrary, however, *that* is too much to believe.
As Harvard law professor Simon Greenleaf, a man who lec-
tured for years on how to break down testimony and determine whether or not a witness was lying, says, "It was . . .
impossible that they could have persisted in affirming the
truths they have narrated, had not Jesus actually risen from
the dead, and had they not known this fact as certainly as
they knew any other fact."

Today the sincere seeker of truth can have complete
confidence, as did the first Christians, that the Christian faith
is based not on myth or legend but on the solid historical fact
of the empty tomb and the risen Christ.

Workout

Increase your power to confront the Stolen Body Myth
with the following:

Read 1 Corinthians 15:1–8. What three things does Paul say are "of first importance"?

that _____

that _____

that _____

How many people (at least) does Paul mention who actually *saw* the risen Christ? _____

What is the significance of Paul's mentioning that most of the five hundred brothers (in verse 6) are still alive?

_____

_____

_____

If five hundred eyewitnesses each gave only five minutes of testimony, it would take forty-two hours just to hear it all. Most trials would only have one or two eyewitnesses give their testimony.

Myths About Religion and Christianity

18

One Man's Ceiling Is Another Man's Floor

B. DOMINEY

Exposing the
Relativity Myth

You can't tell *me* what's right and what's wrong!" Stephanie said. "I'm almost eighteen. You can't push your morals off on me. Just because it's wrong for *you* doesn't mean it's wrong for *me*!" Stephanie stormed out of that confrontation with her parents to find her own version of "right" and "wrong."

Stephanie fell victim to the devil's lie that says, "Right and wrong, good and bad—it's all relative . . . you need to find what's right *for you*, you need to define *your own* morality."

Now, Stephanie's not alone, of course. A lot of people think they can create their own morality, that they invent what is right "for them," what is true "for them."

Allan Bloom, the author of *The Closing of the American Mind*, said in his book that "there is one thing a professor can be absolutely certain of: almost every student entering the university believes, or says he believes, that truth is relative."

But that's a myth. Morality is not relative. Right and wrong are not negotiable. C. S. Lewis, in *Mere Christianity*, stated:

> Whenever you find a man who says he does not believe in a real Right and Wrong, you will find the same man going back on this a moment later. He may break his promise to you, but if you try breaking one to him he will be complaining "It's not fair" before you can say Jack Robinson.
>
> It seems, then, we are forced to believe in a real Right and Wrong. People may sometimes be mistaken about them, just as people sometimes get their sums wrong; but they are not a matter of mere taste and opinion any more than the multiplication table.

The amazing thing is that you don't need a Ph.D. to distinguish right from wrong. The Apostle Paul pointed out that even those who have never heard of the Ten Commandments have "the law . . . written on their hearts, their consciences also bearing witness, and their thoughts now accusing, now even defending them" (Romans 2:15). To quote C. S. Lewis again, "this Law or Rule about Right and Wrong used to be called the Law of Nature . . . because people thought that every one knew it by nature and did not need to be taught it."

And still there are those who insist that what's "wrong" for you isn't necessarily "wrong" for them. But they're not kidding anyone. Their attempt to excuse or explain their conduct with the Relativity Myth betrays the fact that, deep down, they have a sense of right and wrong. They're like Pontius Pilate, who posed the famous question, "What is truth?" (John 18:38). The bitter irony of Pilate's question is that *the* Truth stood before him at that very moment! Jesus, who had revealed Himself as "the Way, the *Truth*, and the Life," embodied the answer Pilate sought, but the Roman governor failed to recognize Truth incarnate.

Workout

Increase your power to confront the Relativity Myth with this workout:

Read Judges 17:6 in the King James Version. The Relativity Myth characterized the days of the judges in Israel, because "every man did that which was _____."

Read Proverbs 14:12. What does this proverb, repeated in Proverbs 16:25, say about the "way that *seems* right to a man"? What result does it bring? What do you think this verse means?

Read Isaiah 45:19. According to this verse, who decides what is right?

Read Hosea 14:9. There are two categories mentioned in the last two lines of this verse. What are they? To which category do you belong? In other words, are you walking in the ways of the Lord, or stumbling in them?

Read John 8:31–32. Does Jesus seem to think there is no absolute of right and wrong, or do His words give the opposite impression? What does He say will be the result of knowing the *truth*?

19

If You're OK, Then I *Must* Be OK

Exposing the God-Will-
Grade-on-a-Curve Myth

Hey, I may not be the greatest person in the world, but I'm not as bad as *him!* Man, I could tell you stories about this guy. We grew up not far from each other and hung around together some, so I know enough about him.

"He was always cocky and arrogant. I kept my mouth shut most of the time.

"He had a police record; I was very cooperative with all the authorities.

"He was in and out of prison; I was never on the wrong side of the law.

"He once even attacked a man right in front of a priest!

"Like I said, I may not be a saint or anything, but I'll tell you one thing—Judas Iscariot isn't as bad as Simon Peter!"

Well, OK, Judas may never have justified himself in quite those words, but all he says above is true. Of course, you know the rest of the story. Judas betrayed Jesus and ended his own life by hanging himself. Peter, although he denied the Lord, repented and was forgiven. He became one of the greatest leaders the church has ever known. But the words we've put in Judas's mouth are not much different from the way some people feel.

"I may have a few drinks now and then," they say, "but I'm not as bad as so-and-so."

Or, "I have my problems, but I don't stab people in the back like her."

Or it may sound more like, "I admit I'm no saint, but if *he's* a Christian, then I should have no trouble getting into heaven."

But that's not the way it works.

Everybody loved the teachers in high school who "graded on a curve." That meant that the teacher would take all the test scores, find the average and award grades according to how many scored above or below that average (of course, there was always some Einstein who threw the curve off for everybody else). But the great part about that system was that as long as everyone else did poorly, you could slack off on the studying and still pull a B.

Some people take that high school experience and project it into their ideas about life and God and righteousness. But the notion that God will grade on a curve is a myth.

The Bible makes it clear that God will not compare Susie to Johnnie and decide, "Well, Susie, you weren't quite as bad as him, so come on into Heaven. Sorry, Johnnie, you have to take what's behind door number three."

On the contrary. A man named Nicodemus once visited Jesus. He was a Pharisee, a member of the Jews' ruling council, a pillar in the community, a man who did all the right things, said all the right things, even believed all the right things. Jesus didn't say to him, "Hey, Nick, if *anybody* is going to get into Heaven, you will!" Jesus said simply, "I tell you the truth, no one can see the kingdom of God unless he is born again" (John 3:3).

It doesn't matter if you're a better person than Jenny Myers. It doesn't matter if you drink less than Abe Landers or go to church more than Scott Jackson. What matters, according to Jesus, is "You must be born again."

Workout

Increase your power to confront the God-Will-Grade-on-a-Curve Myth with this workout:

Read the lines below. Cross out those that are *not* in the Bible:

A. No one can see the kingdom of God unless he is born again.

B. Nobody should seek his own good, but should strive to outdo the good deeds of others.

C. I have fought the good fight, I have finished the race, I have lived a better life than anyone I know.

D. Do not forsake the meetings of the church, for therein you will find salvation.

E. Do not swerve from the paths your friends have set for you.

F. Keep my commandments better than all around you, and you will see the kingdom of God.

G. Believe in the Lord Jesus Christ and bring a greater tithe into the storehouse than your neighbor, and you will be saved, and your household.

H. Unless you repent, you too will all perish.

(*Answers:* A is found in John 3:3. H is found in Luke 13:3.)

20

When the Roll Is Called Up Yonder, Everybody'll Be There

Exposing the
Universalist Myth

Sixteen-year-old Samantha astounded her Sunday school class with the announcement, "The way I figure, Christians, Buddhists, Muslims, it doesn't much matter, y'know? It's like we all want to go to heaven, we're just takin' different roads to the same place."

Samantha may not know it, but many people agree with her. Some don't come right out and say it, but they tend toward universalism, the idea that conscientious devotees of every religion will wind up somehow in heaven. There are "Universalist Churches" that teach this doctrine. Even many (like Samantha) who have been brought up in the church entertain that notion somewhere in the back of their minds.

But it's a myth.

It doesn't jibe with what the Bible teaches. Jesus said, "Enter through the narrow gate. For wide is the gate and broad is the road that leads to destruction, and many enter through it. But small is the gate and narrow the road that leads to life, and only a few find it" (Matthew 7:13–14).

Consider God becoming a man to suffer and die in agony on the cross so men and women can find forgiveness and enjoy eternity in heaven; consider, too, the men and women through the centuries who have accepted or rejected His love; and consider the thousands whose faith in Jesus' atoning sacrifice brought them imprisonment and torture and martyrdom. Then imagine the end of time, when all mankind stands before God. Imagine God surveying the throng of those who have accepted Jesus' dying love on one side and the multitude of those who rejected Him on the other. Then imagine God saying, with a shrug of His shoulders, "Ah, well. Fooey on all that. Everybody c'mon in!"

It won't happen. Not because God wants anybody to face eternity in hell. The Bible says God does not want "anyone to perish, but everyone to come to repentance" (2 Peter 3:9).

The universalist reasons, "I don't see how a loving God could send anyone to hell." But it's not a matter of God sending men and women to hell; He went to elaborate pains to secure eternal life for "whoever believes in him." On the contrary, men and women may spend eternity wherever they choose. The Bible makes it clear that many, stubbornly refusing God's love, will choose eternity in hell.

That is why the Christian must fulfill Christ's command to "go and make disciples of all nations" (Matthew 28:19), because someday, according to the Bible, the opportunity for repentance will be past.

Workout

Increase your power to confront the Universalist Myth with this workout:

Read John 6:68. When many of Jesus' followers were deserting Him, He said to Simon Peter, "You do not want to leave too, do you?" What did Peter reply? What is the implication of his question, "To whom shall we go?" How many roads to eternal life does Peter recognize in this verse?

Read John 14:6. Jesus Himself speaks here about "the way" to heaven. How many roads to God does Jesus recognize in this verse? What is the significance of the article "the" in this verse?

Read Revelation 20:12–15. The Bible plainly prophesies what will happen at the last judgment. According to these verses, will everyone go to heaven? What will happen to those whose names (by their own choice while they lived) are not in the Book of Life?

Take a few moments to thoughtfully and prayerfully follow the directions issued in 2 Corinthians 13:5.

21

It's Not What You Know, It's Who You Know

WILL THE REAL MESSIAH PLEASE STAND!

Exposing the Ideology Myth

Mike and Brandon compared favorite teachers in the registration line at Western Posh University.

"Would you believe I have to take Standish for Western Civ?" Mike moaned. "The guy's a Nazi! At least I got Nelon for English Comp."

"Yeah. I got Christos again," Brandon said.

"Oh yeah? For what class?"

"All of them."

"All of 'em?"

"Yeah."

"Does he give a lot of tests?"

"No."

"You have to memorize his teachings?" Mike asked.

"No," Brandon answered.

"Well, then, what *do* you have to do for this guy?"

"Just mainly get to know him. He wants us to get to know him, to know who he is, and, um, develop a relationship with him."

Hard to imagine a teacher like that, isn't it? But there is one.

Many people entertain the idea that Christianity, like almost any other world religion, is basically a system of beliefs—you know, a set of doctrines or a code of behavior, a philosophy, an ideology.

But that's a myth.

Christianity is not at all like Buddhism or Islam or Confucianism. The founders of those religions said (in effect), "Here is what I teach. Believe my teachings. Follow my philosophy." Jesus said, "Follow me" (Matthew 9:9).

Leaders of the world's religions said, "What do you think about what I teach?" Jesus said, "Who do you say I *am*?" (Luke 9:20, emphasis added).

The question that most religious devotees must ask is, "What ideology do I profess?" The question the would-be Christian must ask is, "What shall I do, then, with Jesus who is called Christ?" (Matthew 27:22).

Christianity is not a religion. It is a relationship.

Christianity is not a system of beliefs or doctrines. It is a Person.

That is precisely why the trial of Jesus is unique. In most trials, the accused is tried for something he or she *did*. Jesus, however, was tried for *who He was*.

In Mark's record of Jesus' trial before the Sanhedrin, he mentions that several false witnesses were produced, but their testimony was conflicting and inconclusive. Then, Mark reports, "the high priest asked [Jesus], 'Are you the Christ, the Son of the Blessed One?'"

Then Jesus, responding to the phrase "Blessed One," which in the Jewish mind was a direct reference to God, said "I am."

At that, the high priest, without waiting for a verdict from the Sanhedrin, tore his robe, indicating that Jesus had blasphemed and had claimed to be God.

The issue at the trial of Christ was His identity—who He was. That is a key difference in Christianity. It is not an ideology; it is based on the identity of Christ and requires a relationship with Him.

What gives the Christian faith credibility is Jesus Christ being the Messiah, the Son of God. That's what caused such conflict between Jesus and the Pharisees. The Pharisees thought that strict adherence to the Law, to biblical principles, was most important. Jesus said, in effect, "No, that won't do. Obeying the Law must be an expression of a person's relationship with Me. Obedience to My teachings will not make you a Christian. Only a personal love relationship with Me can do that."

Workout

Increase your power to confront the Ideology Myth with this workout:

Read Matthew 26:63–65. Is the high priest questioning Jesus about what He's done or who He is? What is Jesus' answer? How does the high priest react?

Read Mark 15:37–39. What does the centurion say after witnessing Jesus' death on the cross? Does he refer to Jesus' teaching or to His identity?

Read Matthew 27:41–43. What did Jesus say *about Himself*, according to those who mocked Him in these verses?

22
Check Your Brains at the Door

Exposing the
Intellectual Myth

Waldo strolled down the city sidewalk, lost in thought. He was going to church. He had decided that he had run from God long enough.

I can't stand it any more, he thought. *The guilt, the conviction, the feeling that my life is missing something.*

So he trod toward the stone church on the corner; its spires and towers stretching to the sky.

Beautiful building, he told himself. *Not like these modern glass skyscrapers they keep putting up.*

After walking for blocks, he reached the church. He stood nervously before the huge wooden doors. Finally, with an awkward gulp, he walked up the steps and into the church.

He halted inside the door to let his eyes adjust from sunlight to the subdued lighting of the church.

"Will you be coming in?"

The voice startled Waldo. He hadn't noticed the woman. He turned in the direction from which the voice had come. He saw a small, slightly hunched woman with gray hair gathered in a bun at the back of her head.

"Will you be coming in?" she repeated.

"Uh, yes," Waldo answered. "Yes, I will."

"Your brains, please."

Waldo was sure he misunderstood her. Then she repeated herself and this time her words were very clear.

"Your brains, please, sir."

"My brains?"

"Yes. You're entering the church, aren't you?"

Waldo nodded.

"You've decided to follow Christ? Become a Christian?"

"Yes," he said.

"Well, then you must check your brains here. You won't

be needing them any more. We'll label them with your name. They'll be safe here. Don't worry, this is the way it's done. If you're going to become a Christian, you check your brains at the door."

Waldo's experience is, of course, fictional. But it reflects how many people feel and think about Christian conversion. They think that becoming a Christian requires you to "check your brains at the door," to sacrifice your intellect and ignore your rational processes.

That's a myth.

Many of the greatest minds in history have belonged to Christians. The Apostle Paul. Augustine. Martin Luther. John Calvin. John Bunyan. Deitrich Bonhoeffer. Francis Schaeffer.

Christian conversion does not compromise a person's intellect. It completes it. Becoming a Christian often prompts an "Aha!" reaction, as a person sees pieces of life's puzzle slipping into place.

In his autobiography, C. S. Lewis tells how he avoided and violently resisted the gospel as a young man because he considered Christianity an unintellectual system. His resistance broke, however, and he was "surprised by joy." He found that conversion *ignited* his imaginative and creative powers. He became most famous for his writings, books like *The Screwtape Letters* and the acclaimed six-part Chronicles of Narnia.

Lew Wallace set out to refute Christianity with his powerful intellect and creativity. But the power of the gospel made a believer out of the author of the classic, *Ben-Hur*.

British trial lawyer Frank Morison intended to write a book disproving the resurrection of Jesus Christ. He conducted intensive research, gathered historical evidence, and worked devotedly at his task. Finally, his intellect and work brought him to the unavoidable conclusion that Jesus had risen from the dead! He became a Christian.

The gospel does not require that you check your brains at the door. On the contrary, it demands the full use of your intellect until you can say with the confidence of Paul, "I am not ashamed of the gospel, because it is the power of God for the salvation of everyone who believes" (Romans 1:16).

Workout

Increase your power to confront the Intellectual Myth with this workout:

Read John 8:32; 1 Peter 3:15; Acts 17:2–4.

Also read Acts 17:16–34, the account of Paul's experience in Athens, where he encountered the sophisticated philosophers and thinkers of the Areopagus. Note verse 23. Does Paul ask the Athenians to set aside their intellect? Does he offer to complete their knowledge for them, to fill in something that is missing from their learning?

Among the converts in Athens was a member of the Areopagus, the great judicial council (note verse 34). Who was it?

23
Jeff and the Professor

Exposing the Blind
Faith Myth

Oh, you're a Christian, are you?" The professor stroked his beard with an air of superiority.

Jeff, in his first year of college, swallowed so hard he thought everyone in the lecture hall probably heard the gulp.

"Tell me," the professor continued, "can you —with 100 percent certainty—prove that Jesus rose from the dead?"

Jeff tried to clear his throat, but his answer still came out in a mousey squeak. "Umm, no."

"You see?" The professor pronounced. "Blind faith. Ignorant, irrational, unreasonable faith." He turned to the blackboard and left a humiliated Jeff to sit through the rest of the class with a red face and defeated heart.

As a young man, I would have agreed with the professor. I thought the Christian faith was a blind faith. I set out to examine it, intending to refute Christianity. However, the more I examined historical, biblical Christianity, the more I realized that it is an intelligent faith, a reasonable faith.

Jesus told His followers, "You will know the truth, and the truth will set you free" (John 8:32). He didn't say, "You will ignore the truth." He didn't say, "Don't even worry about the truth." He didn't say, "You just gotta believe in spite of the truth." He said, "You will *know the truth*, and the truth will set you free."

Jesus does not call upon us to commit intellectual suicide in trusting Him as Savior and Lord. He does not expect us to exercise our Christian faith in an intellectual vacuum. The Christian's faith must be a faith based on the evidence.

The professor who challenged Jeff's faith had the idea that if you can't prove something with 100 percent certainty, then it's useless or untrue. He also figured that the Christian faith is a blind faith since such things as the resurrection and Jesus' deity could not be proven with 100 percent certainty.

That's a myth.

We live in a contingent universe. That means that there are very few things that can be proven with 100 percent certainty, except maybe in the area of mathematics.

Car manufacturers can't prove with 100 percent certainty that their new models are safe. But *the evidence* from a battery of grueling safety tests is pretty conclusive.

A jury can't prove with 100 percent certainty that a suspect committed a given crime. Even if they possess a confession, there are contingencies. He may be lying to protect someone. He may have been coerced. But jurors weigh *the evidence* to form a conclusion "beyond a reasonable doubt."

Similarly, neither the resurrection of Christ nor His deity can be proven with 100 percent certainty. But that doesn't mean that the Christian faith is a blind faith. The evidence for the Christian faith is adequate. It is not exhaustive, for that would result in 100 percent certainty. But it is adequate.

The Apostle John wrote in his Gospel, "Jesus did many other miraculous signs in the presence of his disciples, which are not recorded in this book" (John 20:30). What's he saying? He's saying there are many things Jesus did that confirmed Him as the Son of God that were not recorded. The evidence John provides is not exhaustive. "But," he writes in the next verse, "*these* are written that you may believe that Jesus is the Christ, the Son of God, and that by believing you may have life in his name" (John 20:31, emphasis added). In verse 30, John said, in effect, "Look, the evidence isn't exhaustive." "But," he says in verse 31, "it *is* sufficient."

Blaise Pascal, the French mathematician, philosopher, and scientist, said that there is enough evidence for the Christian faith to convince anyone who is not set against it.

But there is not enough evidence to bring anyone into God's kingdom who will not come.

Workout

Increase your power to confront the Blind Faith Myth with this workout:

Read John 20:30–31. Why did John record the evidence of Jesus' identity as Christ and Son of God? How does "life in his name" come? By belief in what (or whom)?

Read Luke 1:1–4. What qualification does Luke give for writing his Gospel account (verse 3)? Notice Luke addresses his Gospel to someone named Theophilus. What does Luke expect his "orderly account" of Jesus' life and teaching to do for Theophilus?

Have you made it your goal to "carefully investigate" the evidence "so that you may know the certainty of the things you have been taught?"

24

Abe Lincoln and the Ten O'Clock Class

Exposing the Unscientific Myth

Just a minute, sir."

I had just finished lecturing at a prestigious West Coast university when a voice came from the back of the auditorium during the question-and-answer session.

"I'm a graduate student in science here," the young man said, "and I personally cannot accept anything that can't be proven scientifically. Can you prove the resurrection of Jesus scientifically?"

"No," I said.

The student chuckled and struck a smug pose.

"Of course," I continued, "you can't even prove your own statement scientifically."

The scientific method of proving something consists of repeating an event in a controlled situation over and over where the event can be observed, data recorded, and a conclusion drawn. Scientific proof is the result of experimentation and observation.

For example, a scientific proof occurs when a man and woman in lab coats enter a laboratory, she with a clipboard and pencil, he with a small white cake of solid clasped in his hand. The man places the white object in a glass tank filled with ordinary tap water. It bobs to the surface. The woman records something on her data sheet.

He again pushes the object to the bottom of the tank. It bobs to the surface. The woman writes again.

He shoves the object to the floor of the tank again. It bobs to the surface. The woman writes.

He repeats. It bobs. She writes.

After performing the event repeatedly in a controlled environment, observing and recording the result, the scientists conclude that Ivory Soap floats. It's been proven scientifically.

The problem is that many people think that if you can't prove something scientifically, it's untrue or unbelievable.

But that's a myth.

The scientific method is not the only way to prove something. If it were, you would not be able to prove that Abraham Lincoln had ever been president of the United States, because you can't repeat that event. It exists only in the past.

Similarly, you can't prove scientifically that you had a "bear" of a history exam last Friday at 10 A.M. You can't repeat it over and over again in a controlled environment where observations can be made and data recorded. It happened once. It's history.

But just because Abraham Lincoln and your ten o'clock class can't be proven scientifically doesn't mean that they didn't happen. They *can* be proven. And the way they can be proven is called the legal historical method or, better, the evidential method.

The evidential method proves an event by examining three kinds of evidence: oral testimony, written testimony, and physical testimony. This is the kind of "proof" that is offered every day in courts of law around the world, and it's the only kind of proof that applies to an event in history.

How can you prove (by the evidential method) that there was a U.S. president named Abraham Lincoln? If eyewitnesses could be found, you would interview people who knew him, who met him and heard him speak—that's oral evidence. You would compile copies of letters he wrote, newspapers that reported his assassination, and books about him—that's written evidence. Finally, you would offer exhibits of physical evidence—his personal pocket watch, photographs of him, his birthplace, even his sugar bowl.

How would you prove your 10 A.M. history exam last Friday? By the evidential method: Your teacher could testify, you could produce the graded, dated test paper (unless, of course, it should be hidden from your parents), and you could acquire the picture snapped by the yearbook photographer while the test was being taken, and so on.

The scientific method is limited. It cannot prove the above events. It cannot prove that Napoleon was defeated at Waterloo. It cannot prove that the bubonic plague claimed 150,000 lives in seventeenth-century London. It cannot prove that Jesus rose from the dead, because it can't repeat the event in a controlled environment, where observation can be made, data recorded, and a conclusion drawn.

However, a historical event can be proven by the evidential method, by producing oral, written, and physical testimony that establishes the truth of an event beyond a reasonable doubt.

The idea that Jesus' resurrection, for example, is untrue or unbelievable because it can't be proven scientifically is a myth. The life and ministry of Jesus, His miracles, and His resurrection can be proven—and have been—evidentially.

Workout

Increase your power to confront the Unscientific Myth with this workout:

Read John 20:1–9. What physical evidence of Jesus' resurrection is referred to in these verses?

Read John 20:10–29. In these verses, John records the reactions of how many eyewitnesses to the resurrection?

Read John 20:30–31. What kind of evidence is referred to in this verse?

Finally, read 1 Corinthians 15:3–8. How many witnesses of the resurrection does this written account cite?

Considering the evidential method, what other evidence might exist for Christ's resurrection?

25
Stewed Tomatoes and Tennis Shoes

Exposing the Brainwash Myth

Many people have the impression that Christian conversion is a psychologically induced experience brought about by brainwashing the subject with persuasive words and emotional presentations of Christian "myths." They imagine the Christian life to be a delusion. In other words, Christians fool themselves and others with elaborate mind games that produce some changes in behavior.

That's a myth.

I was giving my testimony during a debate in a history class. As I was finishing, the professor spoke up.

"Look, McDowell, we're interested in facts, not testimonies. Why, I have met scores of people around the world who have been transformed by Christ."

"Thank you," I said. "Let me wrap up what I'm sharing, and then I'll concentrate my remarks on your statement."

A few moments later, I addressed the teacher's objection. "Many of you are saying, 'Christ changed your life—so what?' I'll tell you 'so what.'

"One thing that has confirmed to me the resurrection of Jesus Christ two thousand years ago is the transformation of the lives of millions of people when they become related by faith to the person of Jesus. Although they are from every walk of life and from all the nations of the world, they are changed in remarkably similar ways. From the most brilliant professor to the most ignorant savage, when one puts his trust in Christ, his life begins to change.

"Some say it is just wishful thinking, or they simply excuse it by saying it doesn't prove a thing. For a Christian, however, behind his subjective experience there is an objective reality as its basis. This objective reality is the person of Jesus Christ and His resurrection.

"For example," I told the class, "let's say a student comes into this room and says, 'Guys, I have a stewed tomato in my right tennis shoe. This tomato has changed my life. It has given me a peace and love and joy that I never experienced before. Not only that, but I can now run the hundred-yard dash in ten seconds flat.'"

I smiled at the class.

"It's hard to argue with a student like that," he went on. "*If* his life backs up what he says—especially if he runs circles around you on the track. A personal testimony is often the subjective argument for the reality of something. Therefore, *don't dismiss a subjective experience as being irrelevant.*

"However, there are two tests I apply to a subjective experience. First, what is the objective reality for the subjective experience? Second, how many other people have had the same subjective experience from being related to the objective reality?

"If you apply those tests to the stewed tomato in the tennis shoe, what happens? To the first question, he would reply: 'a stewed tomato in my right tennis shoe.'

"The second question would be put this way: How many people in this classroom, in this university, this country, on this continent, and so on, have experienced the same love, peace, joy, and increased track speed as a result of a stewed tomato in their right tennis shoes?"

Most of the students reacted to the question with laughter. Who can blame them? It was obvious that the answer to the second question was "No one!"

What happens, however, when those two tests are applied to the Christian experience?

1. What is the objective reality or basis for my subjective experience—a changed life?

**Answer: the person of Christ and His resur-
rection.**

2. How many others have had this same subjective
   experience from being related to the objective
   reality of Jesus Christ?

   **Answer: millions, from all backgrounds,
   nationalities, and professions have had their
   lives elevated to new levels of peace, joy, and
   victory by turning their lives over to Christ.**

The experience of Christian conversion is no brainwash
job. Although it is subjective, the Christian experience is
based on an objective reality and has been dramatically
repeated innumerable times in the lives of all kinds of people.
The Apostle Paul, in fact, referred to the dynamic power of
the Christian experience when he wrote to the Corinthians,
telling them:

> Do not be deceived: Neither the sexually immoral nor
> idolaters nor adulterers nor male prostitutes nor homo-
> sexual offenders nor thieves nor the greedy nor drunk-
> ards nor slanderers nor swindlers will inherit the
> kingdom of God. *And that is what some of you were.* **BUT**
> you were washed, you were sanctified, you were justified
> in the name of the Lord Jesus Christ and by the Spirit of
> our God.
>
> *1 Corinthians 6:9b–11 (emphases added)*

Workout

Increase your power to confront the Brainwash Myth by
reading the following portions from Acts and indicating the
name, nationality, and profession of the person whose life
was changed through faith in Christ. The first has been
done.

	Name	Nationality	Profession
Acts 8:26–39	unknown	Ethiopian	government official
Acts 9:1–9, 17–19			
Acts 10:1–45			
Acts 16:11–15			
Acts 16:22–33			

26
No Doubt About It

Exposing the
Thomas Myth

Thomas has been the victim of a lot of bad press. OK, so his reputation isn't as bad as Judas, who betrayed Jesus. He might not even rank with Peter, who denied the Lord three times on the eve of His crucifixion. But Thomas is usually classed among the "bad boys" of the disciples, the twelve men who were closest to Jesus during His three years of ministry.

Thomas owes that "bad boy" reputation to an incident following Jesus' resurrection. Jesus had appeared to the disciples behind closed doors. But Thomas was not with them. When they reported to Thomas the news of Jesus resurrection, he responded, "Unless I see the nail marks in his hands and put my finger where the nails were, and put my hand into his side, I will not believe it" (John 20:25).

When Jesus later appeared to Thomas, the Lord said, "Put your finger here; see my hands. Reach out your hand and put it into my side. Stop doubting and believe" (John 20:27).

Many people, however, when they read those words, come down hard on Thomas because of his doubt. In so doing, they forget that none of the other disciples believed until they, too, had seen evidence of the resurrection. Everyone else had already seen Jesus' hands and side. What's more, Jesus didn't say to Thomas, "You should never have doubted." Instead, He showed His disciple the evidence and then said, "Stop doubting." And finally, when Thomas did see the evidence (the Bible doesn't say whether or not he touched Jesus as he had insisted as necessary), he uttered one of the great confessions of faith in history, calling Jesus "my Lord and my God!"

For some reason, we've let ourselves think of doubt as a four-letter word (count 'em—there're five). "*Real* Christians don't doubt," we say.

That's a myth.

Doubt is not the opposite of faith; it is the forefather of faith. Doubt does not cancel faith; it should give way to faith. In fact, as in Thomas's case, doubt can be the impetus that leads us to the truth.

"There lives more faith in honest doubt," said Tennyson, "believe me, than in half the creeds."

Gordon and William Brown, writing in their book, *Romans: Gospel of Freedom and Grace*, observed, "Faith grows through seeking truth, and the seeker must ask questions, and questioning implies 'honest doubt.' The original meaning of the Greek word for 'doubt,' *skeptikos*, is 'inquirer.'"

The Thomas Myth, that "real Christians don't doubt," does not come from the Bible. The lessons to be learned from Thomas's experience are that doubt is natural, that we can be honest about our doubts, and that honest doubt should give way to faith when Jesus reveals the truth to us.

Workout

Increase your power to confront the Thomas Myth with this workout:

Read Luke 24:1–12. What was the disciples' reaction when the women related the news of Jesus' resurrection (verse 11)?

Read Luke 24:13–24. How did these two men on the road to Emmaus react to the news they had heard of the resurrection? Do these verses imply certainty or uncertainty?

Read Luke 24:25–35. How did these two disciples become absolutely convinced of the reality of the resurrection?

Read Luke 24:36–47. What was the first reaction of the disciples to the appearance of the risen Christ (verse 41)? How were they convinced (verses 40, 42, 43, and 45)?

Read John 20:19–29. What was Jesus' response to Thomas's cry, "My Lord and my God?" Similarly, Jesus wishes for us to come to the point of response where we confess Him as Lord and God.

What are your doubts? Pray that Jesus will guide you, through your doubts, to a new confession of faith.

27
Potted Plants Don't Answer Prayer

Exposing the Subjective Faith Myth

Kelly sat at the kitchen table with her friend, Heather.
"I think we each have the faith that's right for us. I mean,
Christianity isn't all there is. The important thing is, that *you
believe*."

Heather puckered her brow as if that would help her
think more clearly.

"I guess," she said. "After all, Christianity is all about
being saved by faith. So I guess . . ." She paused, then started again, speaking slower. "So I guess it's not that big a deal
what you believe, as long as you believe it enough."

Sorry, Heather. Sorry, Kelly. That's a myth.

A college professor recently said to his class, "I believe
in faith. I believe in the power of faith. I've seen it change
lives."

But that's existentialism, not Christianity. Existentialism
stresses "believing," not necessarily what—or whom—is
believed.

I was invited to debate the head of the philosophy
department at a large university on the Marxist theory of
humans as economic creatures. I remarked that the resurrection of Jesus was crucial to me as a person adhering to historical, biblical faith.

"Look, McDowell," my opponent interrupted, "the
issue is not the resurrection. It doesn't matter if the resurrection happened or not. The important thing is—do you
believe it happened?"

"Sir," I answered. "That's wrong. The truth of what I
believe *does* matter, because if what I believe is not true, then
I have no right to my Christian faith."

After the debate, a Muslim student approached me.

"Mr. McDowell," he said, "I know some Muslims who

have more faith in Mohammed than some of you Christians have in Christ."

"That might be true," I said, "but that's not the issue. The issue is not *how much faith you have*, but *who do you have faith in?*"

The value of faith is not in the one doing the believing, but in the one who is believed. You may have more faith than anyone in history, but if you put your faith, for example, in the potted plants in your living room, do you have a saving relationship with God? Do you have forgiveness of sin? Why not, if you're believing enough? Because the object of your faith is a potted plant!

On the other hand, if you have faith the size of freckle, and you put that faith in Jesus Christ, do you have a saving relationship with God? Do you have forgiveness of sin? Definitely. What made the difference? The object of your faith, the One you put your faith in—that's what made the difference.

The Christian faith is not a subjective faith, it's wholly objective. That's why the Apostle Paul stated in 1 Corinthians 15:17, "If Christ has not been raised, your faith is futile; you are still in your sins." Paul recognized that subjective faith—no matter how *hard* you may believe—is insufficient to save you from sin. But when your faith is placed in the risen Jesus Christ, you are saved "by grace . . . *through* faith" (Ephesians 2:8, emphasis added). Faith does not save you; Jesus Christ does.

Workout

Increase your power to confront the Subjective Faith Myth with this workout:

Read John 3:16. Note the importance of the two words "in him" to the message of eternal life in this verse.

Read John 8:24. In this verse, is Jesus emphasizing the importance of *believing* or of believing *in Him*?

Read Acts 16:30–31. What (or in whom) did Paul tell the Philippian jailer to believe?

Look up Romans 3:22 and fill in the crucial words in the following: ". . . righteousness from God comes through faith _____ _____ _____ to all who believe" (Romans 3:22).

28

Sin, Sham, and Billy Graham

Exposing the Elmer Gantry Myth

E lmer Gantry was the title hero of a famous novel by Sinclair Lewis. Gantry, a greedy, lustful, and hypocritical evangelist, preached one thing and practiced another. His words, his sermons, and his life were a sham.

The fictional Elmer Gantry has been paralleled in recent years by scandals that have ruined several famous preachers and ministers. Jim Bakker of "PTL Club" fame was disgraced by revelations of extramarital sex and subsequent cover-ups of the scandal. Jimmy Swaggart's condemnations of Bakker crashed down around him when he was forced to confess to pornographic sin. The media attention given to these and other scandals has led to increased acceptance of the Elmer Gantry Myth, that the majority of preachers and evangelists and Christian leaders are crooked and hypocritical.

The newspaper, magazine, and television coverage of such events, however, doesn't mention the evangelists and preachers who continue to serve God with integrity and humility. Jimmy Swaggart's sin and his struggle to reclaim his shattered ministry seemed to overshadow the fifty-year evangelistic career of Billy Graham. Graham's preaching has reached millions, and his life has never contradicted his preaching. Even so, Graham confesses that from the beginning of his years of ministry, "I was frightened—I still am—that I would do something to dishonor the Lord."

Billy Graham, Luis Palau, Charles Colson, Dawson McAllister, and Charles Swindoll exemplify the vast number of Christian leaders whose lives reflect their teaching. Our society seems to have bought into the Elmer Gantry Myth, that the ranks of preachers and ministers are riddled with hypocrites. But that's a myth.

Peter warned Christians in the first century, "There will be false teachers among you." He also said that these people would "bring the way of truth into disrepute" (2 Peter 2:1–2). That is why the devil works so hard to spread the Elmer Gantry Myth. He wants to bring the truth into disrepute. He wants the preaching of godly men and women to be compromised by the sin and hypocrisy of others.

Regardless of what others may do, however, truth is truth. Salvation is still by grace through faith in our Lord Jesus Christ. God still has the power to "keep you from falling and to present you before his glorious presence without fault and with great joy" (Jude 24).

"Therefore," as Peter says, "be on your guard so that you may not be carried away by the error of lawless men and fall from your secure position. But grow in the grace and knowledge of our Lord and Savior Jesus Christ. To him be glory both now and forever! Amen" (2 Peter 3:17–18).

Workout

Increase your power to confront the Elmer Gantry Myth with this workout:

Read Philippians 1:15–18. What does Paul say about those who seem to preach the gospel falsely? What does he consider "the important thing?"

Read 2 Corinthians 11:3–15. Paul feared that the Corinthians would be led astray because of some people "masquerading as apostles of Christ." Why does Paul say it's not surprising that this should happen?

Read 1 Corinthians 4:16–17. Paul's behavior was such that he could actually tell others to imitate him! What made him confident enough to say that? (Hint: see verse 17.)

Even as we see visible Christian leaders involved in scandals, Paul offers a warning to us. Read 1 Corinthians 10:12. How does this verse say these tragedies should affect us?

29

The Serpent's Promise

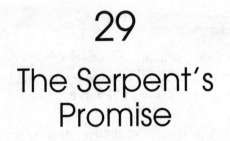

Exposing the New Age Myth

A straight-faced woman in curlers tells her friend in the grocery store about the amazing healing powers of her "mystical quartz crystals." "I haven't had a sniffle or a headache in over a year," she proclaims.

A quiet, good-looking man claims he can communicate with numerous species of animals (whales, dolphins, birds) with musical notes and patterns.

An attractive executive uses ancient Chinese principles to make her business decisions, and a seventy-one-year-old lady "remembers" being a Roman Catholic nun in the eleventh century.

Gurus, extraterrestrials, hypnotism, astral projection, eastern philosophy—the New Age movement (called NAM for short) is a smorgasbord of ideas and beliefs made most famous, perhaps, by Shirley MacLaine's book (and television mini-series) *Out on a Limb*.

What is commonly referred to as the New Age movement is not an organized religion or group of any kind; it is a trend, an emerging school of thought that takes many forms. Although it is impossible to simply state what the NAM is, one of the beliefs that often characterizes New Age thinking is that God is in everything, we are all God, and that by transforming our consciousness, we can discover the "god" (and therefore the unlimited potential) in us.

That's a myth.

The New Age movement, for all its current popularity and television mini-series and best-selling books and business seminars, is nothing new. Some of it dates back to the Garden of Eden.

The Genesis account relates how Satan, in the guise of a serpent, promised Adam and Eve that if they ate the forbidden fruit they would "be like God, knowing good and evil." But Satan, the inventor of the half-truth, lied. Although they did know good and evil (up to that point, of course, they had known only good), they did not become like God.

The New Age movement is evidence that men and women are still making the same mistake. Four hundred years ago, Montaigne remarked, "Man is certainly crazy. He could not make a mite, and he makes gods by the dozen."

God's Word, however, explodes the New Age Myth with the news that Jesus, "being in very nature God, did not consider equality with God something to be grasped, but made himself nothing, . . . and being found in appearance as a man, he humbled himself and became obedient to death— even death on a cross!" (Philippians 2:6–8).

The matchless message of the Bible is not that men can become gods, but that God became man and died for our sins so that we can have eternal life.

Workout

Increase your power to confront the New Age Myth with this workout:

Read Genesis 3:1–7. What was Satan's twofold promise to Adam and Eve if they ate the fruit (verse 5)? Which of these promises was fulfilled when they did eat (verse 7)? What about the promise that they would be like God?

Read the experience of Paul and Barnabas in Acts 14:8–18. How did the crowd react to the healing that they performed (verse 11)? How did these two great missionaries respond when the crowd acclaimed them as gods (verse 14)? What might Paul and Barnabas have said to the claim of the New Age movement that we can become gods by transforming our consciousness?

Read Acts 12:21–23. How did the crowd react to Herod's speech (verse 22)? What then happened to the "god" they acclaimed (verse 23)?

30

Hey, I Don't Deserve This!

Exposing the Rose Garden Myth

Cindy, a seventeen-year-old Christian, is driving home late Friday evening from her part-time job at a restaurant. She stares transfixed as a car from the other side of the highway crosses the center of the road and heads directly for her. She swerves, but the other car collides with her Chevrolet. Cindy is killed on impact. The driver of the other car was drunk.

A hornet stings two-year-old Faith as she is playing in her backyard. Her face swells immediately. Her mother recognizes the severity of the reaction, but before they arrive at the hospital, Faith dies. Her parents had no idea she was acutely allergic to bee stings.

A baby is born to a lower-caste woman in India. He spends all four months of his life in a cardboard box before he dies of starvation. His mother dies two months later.

Life isn't fair. Babies die. Good people suffer. Christians hurt terribly. And good people who suffer often respond, "Hey! I don't deserve this! It's not fair. Why me?"

People have asked that question for generations, from the ancient patriarch Job, whose story is found in the Bible, to Rabbi Harold Kushner in his book, *When Bad Things Happen to Good People*.

The question springs from the idea that good people, Christians particularly, are entitled to lives that are free from struggle and sorrow and suffering.

But that's a myth.

God never promised Christians a rose garden. He never said that life would be easy and that only good things would happen to good people. He doesn't guarantee a life of comfort and ease for people who love and serve Him.

Admittedly, that's what people have assumed for millennia. But a careful reading of God's Word shows the fallacy of that statement.

Jesus' disciples asked Him the age-old question about why people suffer. They pointed to a man who had been born blind.

"Rabbi," they asked Him, "who sinned, this man or his parents, that he was born blind?"

Jesus responded, "Neither," and healed the man.

That is the case with much of the suffering in the world. Some people suffer because of their sin, like the man who robs a store and is imprisoned for it. Others suffer from the sins of others, like the deformed baby of a cocaine addict. But much of the suffering in the world fits the category of "neither."

When God created the world, He created natural laws such as the law of gravity and laws of motion. We are the beneficiaries of those laws. But we are also occasionally their victims. Sometimes the law of gravity pulls a plane full of people to the ground. Sometimes the laws of motion produce tragic results when automobiles collide. God does not suspend those natural laws for good people.

Life isn't fair. Accidents, diseases, tragedy, death—all these things happen to Christians, too. In fact, one of the most frequent promises Jesus ever made to His disciples was "In this world you will have trouble." But Christians also have the assurance, "But take heart! I have overcome the world" (John 16:33).

Christians are not exempt from suffering; they are, however, equipped for it by the presence of the One who said, "I am with you always, to the very end of the age" (Matthew 28:20).

Workout

Increase your power to confront the Rose Garden Myth with this workout:

Read the following Scripture passages. Identify the person or people who suffer. Why did they suffer? Did God exempt them from suffering or sorrow? What (if anything) did He do for them?

Acts 4:1–13, 21

Luke 23:32–43

1 Corinthians 6:4–10

2 Corinthians 12:7–10

Myths About Life and Happiness

31

Lifestyles of Rich
and Amos

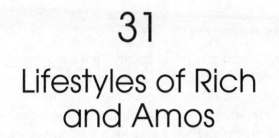

Exposing the
Consumer Myth

Man, he had it all. My friend Rich dropped out of high school. Not because he couldn't cut it. It's just that Rich knew he could make some pretty big money without a diploma. He left the stale-smelling classrooms behind for a factory job that paid high wages for a sixteen-year-old.

That job gave Rich the kind of buying power that I could only imagine. He sloshed through mud in his all-terrain vehicle. He whizzed over snow in his snowmobile. He sped across the lake in his speedboat. He hauled in the money hand over fist.

I must admit I envied him. At first. Then the plant laid him off, and his income evaporated. Rich lost it all—the snowmobile, the boat, the ATV. Worse, his whole life sort of crumbled and lost meaning. He had been so wrapped up in accumulating possessions that "getting" more and more *things* became his purpose in life. As soon as he bought the boat, he began planning his next purchase. Rich had bought into the Consumer Myth, that buying the right things—and enough of them—will bring happiness.

It hits all of us sooner or later. Amos, an eighth-grader, told me recently that he didn't know what career he would choose, but it had to be one in which he could make "a lot of money" and have a fancy car and a downtown apartment.

The advertising industry exists to promote this myth. Television, radio, and magazines tell you repeatedly about all the *things* you can't live without: Swatch, Calvin Klein, Pontiac (We build excitement), Cover Girl, Jordache Basics, Sony, Tres L.A., Bugle Boy, Conair, L.A. Gear, Maybelline, CD players, VCRs, ATVs, RVs, 4WDs, and MTV. Advertisers work hard to convince you that "getting"—and having—*things* is the way to happiness.

But how much money does it take to be happy? What kind of car will fulfill you? If you had everything on your wish list right now, would you dust your hands and say, "Whew! All done," or would you begin a new wish list?

The Sword of the Spirit, God's Word, exposes the Consumer Myth for the lie that it is. Luke records Jesus' warning to "Be on your guard against all kinds of greed; a man's life does not consist in the abundance of his possessions" (Luke 12:15).

Paul, in his letter to the Philippians, sounds like a man who had it made. Whatever it takes to be happy, this guy had it. He exults, "Rejoice in the Lord always. I will say it again: Rejoice!" (Philippians 4:4). Not only that, but his brief letter to the Christians at Philippi mentions "joy" or "rejoicing" *seventeen* times! Paul had it all.

But wait a minute. A quick look at the first chapter reveals that Paul was *in prison* when he wrote all that stuff about joy and happiness (verses 12–14). He had *nothing*, to our way of thinking. No Swatch. No ATV. No Bugle Boys. No Walkman. But he was happy. He said, "I have learned to be content whatever the circumstances. I know what it is to be in need, and I know what it is to have plenty. I have learned the secret of being content in any and every situation, whether well fed or hungry, whether living in plenty or in want. I can do everything through him who gives me strength" (Philippians 4:11–13).

Happiness does not depend on possessions. As a matter of fact, real joy is totally independent of externals. The reason a Christian can be joyful regardless of poverty or riches, stormy seas or smooth sailing, is because of something internal, an inward reality and peace that only comes from Jesus Christ.

Workout

Increase your power to confront the Consumer Myth with this workout:

Read 1 Timothy 6:9. What does it say about the Consumer Myth?

Read 1 Timothy 6:3–5. Paul speaks in these verses of men who think that godliness will pay off financially.

Paul contrasts that with another attitude in verse 6. What does he say is truly "great gain"?

Read Hebrews 13:5. This verse cites one reason to be content with what you have. What is it? What does God's presence have to do with being content?

Read Luke 6:38. What does Jesus say in this verse about greed? Generosity? Is He talking about anything more than money? Now list what you think you really need to be happy. Be honest. How much of it costs money?

32

"The Lip" and the Artful Dodger

Exposing the Leo Durocher Myth

L eo "the Lip" Durocher played shortstop for the Brooklyn Dodgers, New York Yankees, Cincinnati Reds, and St. Louis Cardinals in the 1930s and '40s. He also managed successfully in the majors. But Durocher is, perhaps, most famous for his fiery temper and for a philosophy he used to justify his behavior: "Nice guys finish last."

The feisty Durocher growled and scratched his way to three National League pennants as a manager. His teams often reflected his temperament. He believed that a person had to kick and claw, bite and bump, hit and hurt if he expected to win.

But that's a myth. The Leo Durocher Myth. It might just as easily be called the J. R. Ewing Myth. Or the Angela Channing Myth. Any way you look at it, though, it's a myth.

Orel Leonard Hershiser IV was the pitching ace of the 1988 World Champion Los Angeles Dodgers. He won twenty-three games during the regular season that year. Not only that, he also set a record by pitching fifty-nine consecutive scoreless innings to finish the 1988 season. Not only that, he earned the Most Valuable Player awards for the League Championship Series against the New York Mets and for the Dodgers' World Series victory over the Oakland A's, going 3–0 in the postseason with two shutouts. Not only that, he was also unanimously named the Cy Young Award winner as the National League's best pitcher.

Orel also happens to be a nice guy. And a Christian. After setting the record for scoreless innings, he knelt on the mound in thankfulness to God. In the locker room after the final World Series game, he told a reporter that he had sung hymns to himself in the dugout to calm himself and maintain his concentration. He gave his testimony on national television that night, saying, "This isn't a religious show, but I want to thank God." Although Hershiser suffered a shoulder injury the following season which ended his playing career, his baseball accomplishments remain in the record books as a testimony to his talent and hard work.

If nice guys finish last, how did Orel get to the top of the heap?

The Sword of the Spirit, the Bible, exposes the Leo Durocher Myth for the lie that it is.

The Leo Durocher Myth says, "Nice guys finish last." The Bible says, "Blessed are the meek, for they will inherit the earth" (Matthew 5:5).

The Leo Durocher Myth says, "Kick and claw your way to the top." God's Word says, "Humble yourselves before the Lord, and he will lift you up" (James 4:10).

The Leo Durocher Myth says, "You've got to step on other people to make it to the top." The Sword of the Spirit says, "God opposes the proud but gives grace to the humble" (James 4:6).

The Leo Durocher Myth says, "Toot your own horn. Strut your stuff. If you've got it, flaunt it." Jesus says, "Everyone who exalts himself will be humbled, and he who humbles himself will be exalted" (Luke 14:11).

Sometimes nice guys *do* finish last. Sometimes not-so-nice guys finish last, too. Durocher finished first three times in his career as a major league manager. Twenty-one times he didn't. His teams even finished last on occasion.

But sometimes, as in Orel Hershiser's case, a nice guy's hard work, perseverance, determination, and humility result in a first-place finish. When that happens, the satisfaction increases because it was achieved in the best possible way.

Workout

Increase your power to confront the Leo Durocher Myth with this workout:

Read Genesis 39:1–6. Joseph entered Egypt as a slave, yet he became an important official in the house of Potiphar the Egyptian (and later rose higher, to second-in-command to Pharoah himself). How did Joseph make it to "the top"?

Read 2 Samuel 1:1–12. This records events that led to David's becoming king of Israel. How did he feel about finally making it to "the top"?

Read Luke 14:7–11. Jesus' parable not only shows great wisdom but also common sense. How can you paraphrase the message of this parable? "Better to think yourself _____ and be proven wrong than to think yourself _____ and be proven wrong."

33
No Geeks, Dorks, or Dweebs

Exposing the
Pharisee's Myth

You'll find them walking the halls of high schools all over America. Dweebs, Grease Monkies, Skinheads. The names may change (depending on whether you're in Los Angeles or Des Moines), but the idea stays the same. There's the right crowd, and then there's the wrong crowd. And you must be careful not to associate with the wrong crowd.

The following quick reference list may help you distinguish between the "right crowd" and the "wrong crowd":

Dweebs, Geeks, Dorks, Nerds: Tacky, mismatched clothes (I mean, plaids with stripes?). Boys wear bow ties and/or pants three inches too short. Pocket protectors. They actually *like* math and science.

Skinheads, Hardnoses, GI Joes: The ROTC type. Fascinated by firearms. Can't wait for the next war. Watch reruns of "Combat!" and "The Rat Patrol."

Grease Monkies, Auto Nuts: They always refer to a car as "this baby," as in "This baby can do zero to sixty in eight seconds." Talk in numbers ("Yeah? Well, *this* baby's got a 454 under the hood").

Jocks: The stereotypical jock can perform pirouettes on the playing field, memorize mammoth playbooks, and cite statistics like a computer. Remove him from the field, though, and he appears to have the intelligence of a doorknob.

Of course, many more can be catalogued: Airheads, Preppies, Bible-Thumpers, Druggies. The point is there are people you can afford to be seen with and there are people you can't be caught dead with! The reasoning is this: If you're seen actually being friendly with a dweeb, some of that "dweebness" may rub off on you. Or at least some people will associate *you* with *them*. And you can't have that, can you?

Jesus had the same problem. He was a rabbi. There were certain people with whom rabbis rubbed shoulders; basically, other rabbis and "extremely religious" people. The Pharisees, especially, devised strict guidelines outlining the right crowd and the wrong crowd. But Jesus broke those rules. He associated with the wrong crowd. He ate with tax collectors. He touched lepers. He talked to a Samaritan woman (a double no-no).

As a result, Jesus was ridiculed and criticized. He showed such disdain for the Pharisee's Myth that He was called "a glutton and a drunkard, a friend of tax collectors and 'sinners'" (Luke 7:34).

Jesus was unaffected by their scorn, however. In the end, it turned out that many of His most loyal friends came from the wrong crowd. Matthew, a despised tax collector, was among His twelve closest disciples. The poor blind beggar whom Jesus healed actually stood up to the Pharisees and courageously testified about Jesus. And Mary Magdalene, from whom Jesus had cast out seven demons, was one of the few who did not desert Jesus through the crucifixion.

Who knows? Maybe a friend is waiting to be discovered among the dweebs, skinheads, and grease monkies at your school. Sure, it may cost you. It will also reward you.

After all, Jesus said to you, "I have called you friends. . . . You did not choose me, but I chose you and appointed you to go and bear fruit—fruit that will last. Then the Father will give you whatever you ask in my name. This is my command: Love each other" (John 15:15b–17).

Workout

Increase your power to confront the Pharisee's Myth with this workout:

The Gospels reveal Jesus as a popular party and dinner guest. Read the following scripture portions and note the people He counted as friends:

Matthew 9:9–13

Mark 14:3

Luke 7:36

Read Luke 19:1–10. Although Jesus did not shun "publicans" and "sinners," He did not participate in their behavior. In Jesus' acquaintance with Zacchaeus, who influenced whom? What application does that have to you and your situation?

34
Boys Will Be Boys

Exposing the
Manhood Myth

Take it from me, conversations in boys' high school locker rooms aren't usually the kind you'd want your mom to hear.

Jock flips his towel at you. "Hey Dan, my man, how'd the date with Andrea go Friday night?"

Guy beside you elbows you in the ribs. "Hit the jackpot?"

Someone else, "Is she hot or what?"

"She serve you breakfast the next morning?"

Followed by cackles, gestures, swaggers, and caveman comments like, "Yow!" and "Baby, baby!" and "Ooo mama!"

But a lot of guys know the pressure of that locker-room situation. Even if you don't actually say so, you *have* to give the impression that you "scored," that you've "done it," that you've had sex. If you don't, you're a wimp. Sex is like a rite of passage. You're not a man unless you've had sex.

That's a myth. It's a lie of the devil.

As I put it to thousands of young people across the country in the national Why Wait? campaign, "What does having sex have to do with being a man? A twelve-year-old kid can have sex!" I said. "It takes a man to say no."

I went on to say, "It takes boldness to be right up front and say, 'Look, I don't want to be sexually involved right now.' Virginity is actually something to be proud of, not ashamed of!"

Having sex is relatively easy. It doesn't take maturity or strength of character. Taking a stand alone in the face of a crowd is hard. *That* takes character, strength, and guts.

You may not realize it, but the Bible records some pretty nitty-gritty accounts of sexual temptation and sin. One of them involves Joseph.

Joseph worked for a high Egyptian official named

Potiphar. The Bible says, frankly, "Now Joseph was well-built and handsome, and after a while his master's wife took notice of Joseph and said, 'Come to bed with me!'"

Joseph could easily have allowed himself to be seduced. Maybe then he could've strutted around the locker room and bragged about his conquest! It was a chance to prove himself to be a "man."

"But he refused," the Bible says. More than once, in fact. And as a result, his refusal of her amorous advances landed him in prison. But Joseph had character, strength, and guts. Joseph—now there was a man.

It takes a man like that to stand up to locker-room pressure. It takes a man to summon the strength to follow his conscience. It takes a man to refuse to conform to the crowd. It takes a man to say no.

Workout

Increase your power to confront the Manhood Myth with this workout:

Read Genesis 39:1–9. Joseph had the opportunity to go to bed with Potiphar's wife. What was his response (verse 8)? He gave two reasons for his decision (verses 8–9). What were they?

Read Genesis 39:10. How often did Joseph have to face that temptation (verse 10)? How did he try to avoid the temptation (verse 10)?

Read Genesis 39:11–23. When he found himself alone with Potiphar's wife and tempted by her again, how did Joseph respond (verse 12)? Joseph was even punished as a result of his virtue, but what blessing came to him because of his refusal to sin against God (verses 20–23)?

35
The Crossing Guard

Exposing the Egoist Myth

You moron! I don't care how you have to do it, you get those charts and figures for me NOW!"

Rachel Townsend slammed the telephone into its cradle and bellowed her secretary's name. The plush upholstery and dark woodgrain walls of her office attested to her importance. The book on the corner of her desk reflected her attitude: *Looking Out for Number One*. Rachel had risen rapidly in the company by ruthlessly promoting herself and her own interests above everyone else. She was not embarrassed that she had "stepped on" other people to achieve her position. She entertained no false modesty. She took secret pride in her own importance.

Her secretary entered the office, and Rachel began spouting orders.

"Get that stupid jerk Patterson in here. And tell Allison to drop whatever she's doing for what's-his-name and start on my files—"

She halted. Something in her secretary's look stopped her.

"Your daughter," the secretary said. "The babysitter called. Danielle's disappeared from her backyard."

Rachel grabbed the phone. She spit questions into the phone like a machine gun. Finally she hung up and barked to her secretary, "Get my ex-husband. Tell him to get over to the sitter's NOW."

Rachel flung herself into the bucket seat of her BMW and spun out into the street. Honking, darting, dodging, she sped toward the sitter's house. *If anything happens to her, I'll kill myself.* She ran a red light. *What if I don't find her? I'll need help.*

The car careened around a corner. *Who would help me?* The thought terrified her. *Who would help me?*

Rachel realized that, because she had always been the center of her universe, she had no one to help her, no one to turn to. *I guess I thought I'd never need anyone. I've always acted like no one else was important . . . just me.*

She was almost there now. She slowed only slightly as she approached the intersection and saw the crossing guard just in time to slam on her brakes. Fury erupted in her like a volcano. She recognized this crossing guard who shuffled in the crosswalk, his back to her. He had been on that corner for years, waving to cars, crossing schoolchildren. He'd always seemed, to Rachel, a doddering, insignificant old man. And now he had forced her to screech violently to a stop and lose precious time. She opened her mouth to fling curses at him when she noticed he had a child in his arms—her child, Danielle!

Rachel swung her door open and ran hysterically to the man. She grabbed her smiling three-year-old from his arms and hugged her, overcome with gratitude. Rachel, the corporate executive, felt strangely small.

Suddenly, the old man was important.

Rachel Townsend exemplifies the egoist, a person who thinks that he or she is the center of the universe. An egoist places himself before everyone else. An egoist thinks, *Forget everybody else. As long as I get what I want out of life, I'll be happy.*

But that's a myth.

People who follow that course may sometimes end up wealthy or powerful, but they also reap loneliness and bitterness.

Jesus taught that each of us, even the smallest child, is immensely important in God's eyes. Recognizing the value of those around you will increase your happiness, not diminish it. Jesus reiterated the command, "Love your neighbor as yourself." Not less than yourself. Not more than yourself.

"Love your neighbor as yourself."

The poet Jon Donne also said something like that we he wrote:

> No man is an island, entire of itself;
> every man is a piece of the continent,
> a part of the main . . .
> any man's death diminishes me,
> because I am involved in mankind;
> and therefore never send to know for whom
> the bell tolls; it tolls for thee.

God did not make you the center of the universe. But He does want to be in the center of *your* life.

Workout

Increase your power to confront the Egoist Myth with this workout:

Each of the following Scripture passages identifies an egoist. Answer these two questions regarding each: Who is (are) the egoist(s)? What becomes of him or her?

2 Samuel 15:1–12; 18:17

1 Kings 1:5–6, 42–53

Isaiah 14:3–4, 12–15

Matthew 20:20–28

36

Beauty Is the Beast

Exposing the
Cover Girl Myth

Catherine's cover-girl beauty qualifies her for the pages of *Vogue* or *Mademoiselle*. Her slim figure seems suited for a black evening gown. Her elegance and charm would grace the elite penthouse parties of the super-rich. So what's she doing in a sewer?

Catherine (Linda Hamilton), of the former hit television series, *The Beauty and the Beast*, frequents the underground haunts (abandoned subway tunnels, actually) of Vincent, the manbeast portrayed by Ron Perlmann. Okay, so it's an old story with a new twist. The thing I want to know is, *What's she see in him?*

I mean, really, here's this gorgeous brunette, right off the cover of some magazine, and she's in love with a guy who looks like a lion and lives underground. Get real!

Of course, that's part of the show's appeal. Catherine is attracted to Vincent not because of his appearance, but *in spite* of it. She's in love with the guy under the lion's mane. She loves him for his sensitivity and compassion . . . and maybe for his marvelous voice. And part of the show's charm is that love like that is rare.

That's because too many of us have bought into the Cover Girl Myth. We've actually come to believe that looks *are* everything, that if a girl doesn't look like Elle McPherson or a guy like Patrick Swayze, they're unattractive. But that's a myth.

Television, magazines, movies, and videos constantly drum into us a prepackaged image of what is beautiful and what is not. The media machine also touts the idea that beautiful = happy. Now please understand that Christians aren't obligated to be ugly. But we're not obligated to look like a Jordache or Soloflex commercial either. We need to realize that there's a lot more to beauty than heavenly figures, bulging biceps, and blue eyes. Beauty more often results from a person's attitude and disposition. God chose David to be king of Israel, not because of his appearance or physical attributes, "for the Lord seeth not as man seeth," the Bible says. "For man looketh on the outward appearance, but the Lord looketh on the heart" (1 Samuel 16:7 KJV).

Often, in fact, beauty, as the world defines it, is not a blessing. Incredible as it may seem, sometimes beauty *is* the beast that drives a girl to depression or robs a boy of his self-esteem. There are many "beautiful" people who happen to be lonely, insecure, and unfulfilled.

The truth is, if you're seeking happiness in the color of your hair or the cut of your clothes, you're sure to be disappointed. Clothes are important, for example, but learn to look beyond the reflection in the mirror. Whether you're pleased with the person you see there will have more to do with what you *can't* see than with what you can.

Workout

Increase your power to confront the Cover Girl Myth with this workout:

The Bible repeatedly tells what it takes to find happiness. Read the following verses and note the keys to happiness that are mentioned. List them in the space provided. Then place a check mark beside those that depend on physical characteristics.

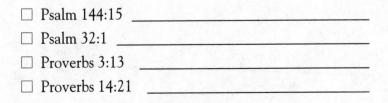

☐ Psalm 144:15 _____

☐ Psalm 32:1 _____

☐ Proverbs 3:13 _____

☐ Proverbs 14:21 _____

- ☐ Proverbs. 16:20 _____
- ☐ Luke 11:28 _____
- ☐ James 1:12 _____
- ☐ 1 Peter 3:14 _____

37
Everybody's Doing It

Exposing the
Conformist Myth

C'mon, Mom, be reasonable," pleaded Andrea. "There aren't gonna be, like, drugs or anything. It's just a party."

"You're not going to a party at Brad's house—or anyone's house—unless there are some adults present to chaperone."

"I can't believe you're doing this to me," Andrea said. "Everybody else is going to be there. I'll be the only one whose mother won't let her go."

Andrea didn't speak to her mother for the rest of the weekend. *Everybody goes to those kinds of parties these days,* she reasoned. *It's not like when you and Dad were kids.*

Andrea was surprised on Monday morning at school to find out that Julia hadn't gone to Brad's party either.

"My parents wouldn't let me," Julia confessed. "Even Cindy didn't show up."

Andrea supposed that everybody would be at Brad's unchaperoned party. She still wasn't happy with her mom, but she did feel much better about her mom's judgment.

Andrea accepted a common belief: the idea that "everybody's doing it."

But that's a myth.

Everybody's *not* doing it. Sometimes it does seem that way, but a perceptive young person will eventually discover that a lot fewer people are "doing it" than the crowd would have them believe.

Everybody's *not* having premarital sex. My research indicates that more than 50 percent of Christian kids *aren't* "doing it." That's a significant number.

Everybody's *not* using tobacco. Some surveys indicate that as many as 80 percent of youth do not smoke today.

Everybody's *not* using alcohol. Various surveys indicate that around 30 percent of high school students do not use alcohol and nearly 10 percent have *never* tried it.

Everybody's *not* doing drugs. The Institute of Social Research at the University of Michigan reported a sharp drop in the use of cocaine and other drugs by teenagers. Over 40 percent of all American young people have refused illicit drugs all the way through high school graduation.

Everybody's *not* losing or "outgrowing" their faith. A survey of two thousand teenagers shows 61 percent regard religion as the most important part of their lives.

The lie that everybody's doing it is often used by teenagers to manipulate their friends and peers into conforming with the rest of the crowd. Well, don't believe the Conformist Myth. Everybody's *not* "doing it." A hefty percentage of teenagers know how to say no. And they're doing it more and more.

Workout

Increase your power to confront the Conformist Myth with this workout:

In the spaces provided below, list teens you know who are not "doing it" (feel free to include the most important name—*yours!*).

Among the 30–40 percent who're not having premarital sex:

_____

_____

Among the 80 percent who do not use tobacco:

_____

_____

Among the 30 percent who do not use alcohol:

_____

_____

Among the 40 percent who are refusing illicit drugs:

_____

_____

Among the 61 percent who consider their faith the most important part of their lives: _____

_____

38
Sex Is Not a Dirty Word

Exposing the Puritan Myth

One reason for the popularity of Dana Carvey's character, the Church Lady (who became famous on "Saturday Night Live"), is that she reflects how a lot of people see Christianity. The hypocritical, prudish attitude of this lady in her calf-length dress and pulled-back hair characterizes the view that Christians consider sex a four-letter word. In many people's minds, those who follow Jesus believe in a God who condemns sex and sexuality.

That's a myth.

Sex is not a dirty word. It is not wrong, nor sinful, nor shameful.

God does not hate sex. He's the One who invented it! He started the whole thing. The creation account in Genesis says, "God created man in his own image, in the image of God he created him; male and female he created them" (Genesis 1:27). He created man and woman with sexual organs, with full sexuality and natural sensuality. And He looked down on these immensely sexual creatures, and, the Bible says, "God saw all that he had made, and it was very good" (Genesis 1:31).

Sex has been a part of God's plan from the beginning. When He told man and woman, "Be fruitful and increase in number," He meant for them to obey Him through sexual activity.

The Bible contains some pretty frank accounts of sexuality. The Song of Solomon, of course, is a love poem with language that would shock the Church Lady. The Apostle Paul offered nitty-gritty advice on sexual behavior to married couples in the church at Corinth. However, Scripture doesn't mince words about the fact that sex is to be enjoyed between husband and wife. "Marriage should be honored by all," says the writer of Hebrews, "and the marriage bed kept pure, for God will judge the adulterer and all the sexually immoral" (Hebrews 13:4).

God created sex; it is man who has taken it outside of the marriage covenant and defiled it. God intended sex to be a fulfilling, exciting, satisfying experience between a man and woman totally surrendered to each other in the enjoyment of each other's sexuality; it is man who has perverted God's gift.

When God says, "Thou shalt not commit adultery" or sexual immorality, He doesn't do it because He's a cosmic killjoy but rather because He's a celestial lovejoy. God wants to protect you from distrust or suspicion and provide for you one of the most important factors for a fulfilled love, marriage, and sexual relationship, and that is trust.

He wants to protect us from the fear of sexually transmitted diseases and to provide a peace of mind sexually when we enter into marriage.

He wants to protect us from bad relationships that are artificially sustained and often lead into tragic marriages because of sexual involvements.

Finally, He wants to protect our virginity, to provide for us one of the greatest love gifts that a person can present to a mate on their wedding night.

Workout

Increase your power to confront the Puritan Myth with this workout:

Read Proverbs 5:1–23 in a modern version. Notice the contrast the wise writer offers between illicit sex and the rewards of sex within marriage. Notice particularly, in verses 18 and 19, the view of sex between a husband and wife.

Read the sensual lyrics of Song of Solomon 3–5. This love poem depicts the sensual (not all of it sexual) pleasure

God gives a man through his wife, and a woman through her husband.

39

Of Shoes and Ships and Sealing Wax, Of Crabs and Other Things

Exposing the
Anarchist Myth

Herman the crab stormed across the sea floor and under the family rock.

"I want to be free!" he screamed at his father. "I don't see how you can expect me to wear this stupid shell twenty-four hours a day! It's confining! It cramps my style. Some of the kids are going to start an anti-shell protest group, and I'm going to join it!"

His father, Fred the crab, inhaled deeply and placed a heavy claw on Herman's shoulder (crabs do have shoulders, although only other crabs can tell where the shoulder ends and the back begins). Herman rolled his eyes.

"Son," he said, "let me tell you a story."

"Dad, not another . . ."

"It's about Humphrey the human, who insisted on going barefoot to school. He complained that his shoes were too confining. They cramped his style, he said. He longed to be free to run barefoot through the flowers and the grass, through fields and streams. Finally, his mother gave in to him. He skipped out of the house—and you know what happened?"

Herman opened his mouth, but his father continued before he could answer.

"Humphrey the human stepped on the pieces of a broken soda bottle. His foot required twenty stitches, and some other guy took his girlfriend to the prom."

"That's a pretty dumb story, Dad."

"Maybe, Son, but the point is this—every crab has felt this way at one time or another, thinking that life would be so much better if he or she could be completely free of the shell. But that's like a sailor getting tired of the confinement of a ship and jumping to freedom in the sea. He may think that's freedom, but if he doesn't get back to the ship or the shore soon, he'll drown—and what kind of freedom is that?"

Herman pondered his father's words.

"Soon you will shed your shell, Son," he said, thinking how hard it would be to say that five times fast.

The young crab looked surprised.

"Yes, you will," father Fred answered the question in his son's expression. "It's called molting, and all crabs do it as they grow up. But," he said with warning in his eyes, "when that happens, you will be more vulnerable than at any other time in your life. Until your new shell hardens like this one"—he tapped his son's armored back—"you'll have to be much more careful and watchful than usual. You'll be less free without this shell, not more free."

"That's funny, Dad," Herman said. "I never thought of it that way. You mean that some things may seem to limit freedom, but really make greater freedom possible, right?"

Fred the crab draped his mammoth claw over Herman's back. They sidled out from under the family rock.

"How'd you get to be so smart, Son?" he asked.

Workout

Increase your power to confront the Anarchist Myth with this workout:

Many people consider the Ten Commandments and the teachings of Jesus to be confining and restrictive. In reality, however, they make true freedom possible to those who follow them.

Read Exodus 20:1–17. What kinds of freedom might result from obedience to these commandments? (For example, obeying the sixth commandment might provide freedom from sexually transmitted diseases.) List your answers on the next page:

_____

_____

_____

Read Matthew 5:1–12. What freedoms might result from following Jesus' teachings in these verses?

_____

_____

_____

Read John 8:36. Write this verse below:

_____

_____

_____

40

Stars in Your Eyes

Exposing the
Love-at-First-Sight Myth

T here I was, crunched in a crowd of guys around my locker the first day of school, talking about, well, you know,
what guys talk about. When all of a sudden—in she walked.

"I knew the second she glided into that school that she
was the girl for me. Man, she was perfect. Blonde hair cas-
cading onto her shoulders, splashing gleams of light into my
eyes. A tan like she just walked off the beach. A figure that
could reduce a seventeen-year-old guy like me to a stuttering
fool.

"I fell in love. Love at first sight, right? Well, it was for
me, anyway. And, it took a while, but I finally got a date with
that vision of loveliness. Things just kinda happened after
that—we were married, had kids, and lived happily ever
after."

Ahhh, that's how it happens. True love. Love at first
sight. Sometimes you can just look at a girl or a guy and *know*
that you've found your love, your life's mate.

That's a myth. Oh, maybe it happens that way every
once in a while. But it can be dangerous to think that those
exceptions typify true love.

We've come to think of love as primarily a feeling: a rush
of emotion, butterflies in your stomach, stars in your eyes. But
the Bible speaks of love as an action, not simply something
you *feel*, but something you *do*.

Many people imagine love to be like the New World
was to Columbus—you're not looking for it, but all of a sudden, there it is! Love! On the contrary, love is more like a
fragrant flower to a gardener—you plant a seed, and water it,
and nurture it, and weed out the things that threaten it, and
water it some more, and days, weeks, months later, it blos-
soms. And it keeps growing and blooming as long as you feed
and water it.

Failure to understand that may be why so many relationships fail: because nobody is prepared to work at love. Nobody thinks you need to water the seed. Nobody is prepared to weather the storms that threaten to uproot the seedling. Nobody is willing to tend the soil. As a result, not many people ever enjoy the full flower of love.

The Apostle Paul emphasized the active nature of love when he said, "Husbands, love your wives, just as Christ loved the church . . ." How did Christ love the church? "[He] gave himself up for her. . . . In this same way, husbands ought to love their wives as their own bodies. He who loves his wife loves himself. After all, no one ever hated his own body, *but he feeds and cares for it*, just as Christ does the church" (Ephesians 5:25–25, 28–29, emphasis added).

You may still feel that rush of attraction when the blonde with the tan walks in. You may swoon when the captain of the football team notices you. But that's not love. It's exciting, but it's not the same as actively loving someone and watching that love grow and blossom into a fragrant flower.

Workout

Increase your power to confront the Love-at-First-Sight Myth with this workout:

Read 1 Corinthians 13, Paul's famous love chapter. Complete the following characteristics of love, according to the apostle:

Love is _____,

Love is _____ (verse 4).

Love always _____,

    always _____,

    always _____,

    always _____ (verse 7).

Love does not _____,
    does not _____,
    is not _____ (verse 4).
    is not _____,
    is not _____,
    is not _____
    it keeps no _____ (verse 5).
Love does not _____
    but _____ (verse 6).
Love never _____ (verse 7).

Now survey your list. How many of the above characteristics of love are feelings? How many are actions?

41
Self-Serve Salvation

Exposing the
Humanist Myth

Buddy and Nathan stopped in front of the book table in the mall. The man and woman seated behind the table smiled nicely at the boys.

"Let me know if I can help you with anything," the man said.

Some of the materials were free, like the booklet that boldly asserted *Jesus Never Existed*. Others cost money, but the topics like global peace, education, and the separation of church and state sounded pretty good.

"Look at this." Buddy held a thick book entitled *Isaac Asimov's Guide to the Bible*. "I've heard of this guy," he said.

"Yes." The man stood and leaned over the table. "That's an excellent book. It not only reveals little-known facts about the Flood and the parting of the Red Sea, but it reveals a lot of things the Bible *doesn't* tell you. It shows how biblical myth and history fit into the larger picture of man's history."

"Uh huh." Nathan nodded at the man, but took the book from Buddy and laid it on the table. "Let's go," he said.

"What's with you?" Buddy asked when they'd walked a few steps. "Why the big hurry to get away from there?"

Nathan shrugged. "I don't know. Something just wasn't right."

Nathan's reaction was wise. He'd confronted secular humanism, a philosophy that is often hard to recognize, but is nonetheless antagonistic to the Bible, Christians, and the church.

Humanists believe that the world can only be saved by mankind. God cannot save man, they reason, because God does not exist. Religion cannot save man, they say, because religion is a lie. Humanity must not look to heaven for salvation, peace, and fulfillment, but to itself.

Humanists believe that the only hope for personal fulfillment and a better world is in throwing off all religious thinking, and placing "absolute faith in nothing save the 'self' or consciousness of self within them." They sincerely believe that man is capable of delivering himself and his world from all evils without the help of any God.

That's a myth.

The history of mankind adequately illustrates that, for all our technological progress, the human race is not becoming increasingly more benevolent and kind. Humanity is not perfecting peace or eliminating war. Man is not solving all his problems just fine on his own. The evidence in this century alone—two world wars, Hitler, Stalin, the Khmer Rouge, McCarthyism, the KKK, the proliferation of nuclear weapons, refugees from war, famine, and oppression—indicates that hope placed in mankind alone is hope *mis*placed.

Of course, we must strive to erase war and famine, we must fight disease and injustice. But humanity cannot save itself. "Salvation is found in no one else," the Bible says, "for there is no other name under heaven given to men by which we must be saved" (Acts 4:12).

The humanist will be no closer to salvation in the year 2000 than those Paul wrote about in the first century, who "exchanged the truth of God for a lie, and worshiped and served created things rather than the Creator—who is forever praised. Amen" (Romans 1:25).

Workout

Increase your power to confront the Humanist Myth with this workout:

Read Jeremiah 16:20–21. How do these words apply to the Humanist Myth?

Read Psalm 36:1–2. Do these words also apply to the

Humanist Myth? How?

Read Psalm 37:39. What perspective does this verse show on the humanist idea that man can deliver himself?

Read Psalm 62:1–2. What is the significance of the word "alone" in these verses? Why is it repeated? Read these verses again, emphasizing the word "my" each time it occurs.

Read 1 Corinthians 3:11. What perspective does this verse offer on humanism?

42
No Place Like Home

Exposing the Heaven-Is-a-Place-on-Earth Myth

Belinda Carlisle topped the charts not too long ago with the hit song, "Heaven Is a Place on Earth."

Nice song. Poor theology.

She's not the only one singing that song, of course. You've probably heard several versions yourself.

"You know what I think?" (You can't help overhearing the girl on the bus talking to the guy in the leather jacket beside her.) "I think heaven is what you make it, I think it's a state of mind. Don't you?"

You've probably also heard the flip side of that record.

"Listen," says the man with the tattoo to the white-aproned guy in the doughnut shop. "I've been through hell *right here*," he says, poking the counter with a stubby finger. "No hell can be worse than what I've already been through."

Well, that's a myth.

It's true that much in human experience can be so blissful that it's difficult to imagine anything better or higher. It's likewise true that some experiences are so violently traumatic that it seems hell could be no worse.

Nonetheless, the Bible clearly teaches that there exists a *real* heaven and a *real* hell.

Jesus told His followers, "In my Father's house are many rooms. . . . I am going there to prepare a place for you" (John 14:2). He also made it clear that heaven is a place or state much to be desired when He told His disciples, who'd thrilled at being able to cast demons out of people, "Do not rejoice that the spirits submit to you, but rejoice that your names are written in heaven" (Luke 10:20).

And the aging Apostle John, in his vision of heaven and the future that has been preserved as Revelation, the last book in the Bible, provides some details about heaven, describing it as a place in the presence of God, where there will be "no more death or mourning or crying or pain," where God's "servants will serve him. They will see his face. . . . And they will reign for ever and ever" (Revelation 21:4; 22:3–5). To the girl on the bus who thinks heaven is on earth, the message of the Bible might be put, "You ain't seen nothin' yet!"

However, God's Word is likewise clear that the future holds punishment for the wicked in a place or a state that we have come to call hell. Jesus spoke plainly about a time when "he will say to those on his left, 'Depart from me, you who are cursed, into the eternal fire prepared for the devil and his angels'" (Matthew 25:41).

John in his vision also relates the punishment awaiting "the cowardly, the unbelieving, the vile, the murderers, the sexually immoral, those who practice magic arts, the idolaters and all liars—their place will be in the fiery lake of burning sulfur. This is the second death" (Revelation 21:8). Tragically, to the man in the doughnut shop who thinks he's been through hell, the message of the Bible might also be put, "You ain't seen nothin' yet!"

In fact, the Bible fairly harps on the subject of hell, addressing the subject over and over in the severest of terms, much like a brakeless truck on a steep hill blasts its horn to warn of approaching danger.

Unfortunately, not enough people heed the Bible's warnings of hell or its promise of heaven. But as the writer of Hebrews says, "We must pay more careful attention, therefore, to what we have heard, so that we do not drift away. For if the message spoken by angels was binding, and every violation and disobedience received its just punishment, how shall we escape if we ignore such a great salvation?" (Hebrews 2:1–3a).

Workout

Increase your power to confront the Heaven-Is-a-Place-on-Earth Myth with this workout:

Read the following portions of Scripture and, in the spaces provided, jot the names of these four people (the speaker or writer in each passage) who revealed their belief in heaven:

1. Matthew 6:20 _____

2. 2 Corinthians 5:1 _____

3. 2 Peter 3:13 _____

4. Revelation 19:11 _____

Do the same with the following people who reveal their belief in a real hell:

5. Matthew 23:33 _____

6. 2 Peter 2:4 _____

7. Revelation 20:13–15 _____

(*Answers:* 1. Jesus; 2. Paul; 3. Peter; 4. John; 5. Jesus; 6. Peter; 7. John)